FRANK LLOYD WRIGHT LOUIS SULLIVAN AND THE SKYSCRAPER

DONALD HOFFMANN

D1444435

DOVER PUBLICATIONS, INC.
Mineola, New York

EVANSTON PUBLIC LIBRARY
1703 ORRINGTON AVENUE
EVANSTON, ILLINOIS 60201

JAN 2 1 1999

Copyright

Copyright © 1998 by Donald Hoffmann
All rights reserved under Pan American and International Copyright Conventions.

Published in Canada by General Publishing Company, Ltd., 30 Lesmill Road, Don Mills, Toronto, Ontario.
Published in the United Kingdom by Constable and Company, Ltd., 3 The Lanchesters, 162–164 Fulham Palace Road, London W6 9ER.

Bibliographical Note

Frank Lloyd Wright, Louis Sullivan and the Skyscraper is a new work, first published by Dover Publications, Inc., in 1998.

Library of Congress Cataloging-in-Publication Data

Hoffmann, Donald.
    Frank Lloyd Wright, Louis Sullivan, and the skyscraper / Donald Hoffmann.
        p.   cm.
    Simultaneously published in Canada by General Pub. Co. and in the United Kingdom by Constable and Co.
    Includes index.
    ISBN 0-486-40209-6 (pbk.)
    1. Skyscrapers—United States.   2. Wright, Frank Lloyd, 1867–1959—Contributions in skyscraper design.   3. Sullivan, Louis H., 1856–1924—Contributions in skyscraper design.   I. Title.
NA6232.H64   1998
720'.483'0922—dc21   98-18906
                                                                                  CIP

Manufactured in the United States of America
Dover Publications, Inc., 31 East 2nd Street, Mineola, N.Y. 11501

ACKNOWLEDGMENTS

Romantic ideas of the skyscraper will no doubt persist, but they tell little about the true nature of this most refractory of architectural types. Ephemeral data and obscure sources can prove far more valuable. In trying to give an accurate account of the skyscraper and how two famous American architects confronted its inherent problems, I have benefited from the resources of various institutions and the kind help of many persons. Any study of Wright now leads inevitably to the special collections of the Getty Research Institute for the History of Art and the Humanities, Los Angeles, and to the Frank Lloyd Wright Archives in Scottsdale, Arizona, where I am particularly grateful to Bruce Brooks Pfeiffer, director, and Indira Berndtson, administrator of historic studies. The drawings from Wright's studio and the quotations from his correspondence are reproduced by permission of the Frank Lloyd Wright Foundation.

For their help in pursuing Sullivan and the Wainwright Building, I am indebted to April West of the Missouri division of Design and Construction, Jefferson City; Bryce Hastings of Hastings & Chivetta Architects, St. Louis; Cynthia Hill Longwisch of the Landmarks Association of St. Louis, Inc.; Paul Eckardt, maintenance supervisor of the Wainwright Building; J. Dowling, manager of the Chemical Building, St. Louis; Charles Brown, reference librarian at the Mercantile Library Association, St. Louis; the St. Louis chapter of the American Institute of Architects; Suzy Frechette of the St. Louis Public Library; Kirsten Hammerstrom of the Missouri Historical Society, St. Louis; Pamela Paterson of the St. Louis Art Museum; Prof. Osmund Overby of the University of Missouri-Columbia; and Fae Sotham of the State Historical Society of Missouri, Columbia.

For their courtesies in Chicago, I am indebted to Tim Samuelson of the Commission on Chicago Landmarks; Fran Bass and Emily Clark of the Chicago Historical Society; Mary Woolever, architectural archivist, and Robert Cozzolino, assistant archivist, of the Ryerson and Burnham Libraries at the Art Institute of Chicago; Ward A. Miller of Vinci/Hamp Architects; and the staff of the Chicago Public Library.

Elsewhere, I am grateful for the help of Elizabeth Douthitt Byrne, head of the Environmental Design Library at the University of California at Berkeley; David A. Bahlman, executive director of the Foundation for San Francisco's Architectural Heritage; Paul Fisher of San Francisco; the staff of the San Francisco Public Library; Keith Simmons of the University Art Museum, the University of California at Santa Barbara; Jane Nowak of the Los Angeles Public Library; Peter Blodgett, curator of Western Historical Manuscripts, the Huntington, San Marino; Dan Kany and Bill O'Malley at the Avery Library of Columbia University in New York; Marjorie Pearson, director of research for the New York Landmarks Preservation Commission; Edgar A. Tafel, Architect; Prof. James O'Gorman of Wellesley College; Prof. Dietrich Neumann of Brown University; Christopher T. Baer and Lynne Joshi of the Hagley Museum and Library, Wilmington, Delaware; Barbara Bezat, at the Northwest Architectural Archives of the University of Minnesota, St. Paul; Joyce E. O'Donnell, executive director of the Landmark Preservation Council in Bartlesville, Oklahoma; Kathy Triebel, corporate archivist for the Phillips Petroleum Company, Bartlesville; Joe D. Price of Corona Del Mar, California; Will Miller of Portland, Oregon; Mark Heyman of St. Louis; Elizabeth Wright Ingraham, Architect, of Colorado Springs; Richard Helstern, Architect, of Carbondale, Illinois; and Robert Kostka, Ashland, Oregon.

For their encouragement, I am indebted to Prof. William L. MacDonald of Washington, D.C.; my brothers, George Hoffmann, John Hoffmann, and Fred Hoffmann; Elpidio Rocha of Eugene, Oregon; and Ellen Goheen of the Nelson-Atkins Museum of Art in Kansas City, Missouri.

D.H.

CONTENTS

List of Illustrations
VII

Introduction
3

The Engine of Profit
5

The Great Desideratum
9

Sullivan's Dream
17

The Wainwright Building
21

Sullivan and Authenticity
37

Wright and Light
43

Wright's Idea
53

The Anti-skyscraper
63

Notes
83

Index
91

LIST OF ILLUSTRATIONS

1. Wainwright Building, St. Louis. *Photo:* Lester Jones, for the Historic American Buildings Survey. *Courtesy:* Library of Congress. 2

2. Wainwright Building, east front. *Photo:* the author. . . . 3

3. Reliance Building, Chicago, main entrance. *Photo:* from *Ornamental Iron. Courtesy:* The Art Institute of Chicago 4

4. Offices of Adler & Sullivan, Chicago, plans. From the *Engineering and Building Record. Courtesy:* Linda Hall Library 4

5. Masonic Temple, Chicago. *Courtesy:* Chicago Historical Society 6

6. Odd Fellows' Temple project, Chicago. From the *Graphic. Courtesy:* Chicago Historical Society. 7

7. Street view of conjectural setback skyscrapers. From the *Graphic. Courtesy:* Chicago Historical Society . . 8

8. Skyscraper expression. *Diagram:* the author 8

9. Leiter Building, Chicago, detail of east face. *Photo:* Richard Nickel 10

10. Willoughby Building, Chicago, detail of south front. *Photo:* Richard Helstern. 11

11. Marshall Field Wholesale Store, Chicago. *Courtesy:* Chicago Historical Society 11

12. Willoughby Building, interior. *Photo:* Richard Helstern 12

13. A. T. Stewart Store, New York, west front. *Courtesy:* New-York Historical Society 12

14. Fagin Building, St. Louis. From *Commercial and Architectural St. Louis* 13

15. The Rookery, Chicago, light court, looking southwest. From the *Inland Architect. Courtesy:* The Art Institute of Chicago 13

16. The Rookery, light court, looking east. From the *Inland Architect. Courtesy:* The Art Institute of Chicago. 14

17. Tacoma Building, Chicago. *Photo:* Chicago Architectural Photo Company 15

18. Tacoma Building, plan of typical floor. From *Prominent Buildings Erected by the George A. Fuller Company. Courtesy:* The Art Institute of Chicago . . . 16

19. Wainwright Building, south front. *Photo:* Copyright © 1996 Cervin Robinson. 20

20. Wainwright Building, preliminary scheme. From the *St. Louis Globe-Democrat. Courtesy:* St. Louis Public Library. 22

21. Houser Building, St. Louis. From *Commercial and Architectural St. Louis* 23

22. Wainwright Building, rendering. From *The City of St. Louis and Its Resources. Courtesy:* State Historical Society of Missouri 24

23. Wainwright Tomb, St. Louis. *Photo:* the author. . . . 24

24. Wainwright Building in construction. From *Engineering Magazine* 25

25. Typical four-segment Phoenix column, plan and elevation. From *Useful Information for Architects, Engineers and Workers in Wrought Iron and Steel. Courtesy:* Hagley Museum and Library 25

26. Wainwright Building, fireproofed column in attic. *Photo:* the author 26

27. Wainwright Building, basement plan. From *The Wainwright Building. Courtesy:* St. Louis Public Library. 26

28. Wainwright Building, first-floor plan. *Photo:* Richard Nickel 27

29. Wainwright Building, second-floor plan. *Photo:* Richard Nickel 27

30. Wainwright Building, plan of typical floor. *Photo:* Richard Nickel 27

31. Wainwright Building, attic plan. From *The Wainwright Building. Courtesy:* St. Louis Public Library. 27

32. Wainwright Building, outlines of south and east fronts. *Diagram:* the author 28

33. Wainwright Building, drawing by Sullivan for terra cotta panels. *Courtesy:* Avery Library, Columbia University 28

34. Wainwright Building, east front. *Photo:* Richard Nickel 29

35. Wainwright Building, corner office. *Photo:* the author 30

36. Willoughby Building, corner office. *Photo:* Richard Helstern 30

37. Wainwright Building, vestibule. *Photo:* Lester Jones. *Courtesy:* State Historical Society of Missouri 31

38. Wainwright Building, seventh-floor corridor. *Photo:* Myra Borchers, for the Historic American Buildings Survey. *Courtesy:* Library of Congress 31

39. Wainwright Building, seventh-floor doors and paneling. *Photo:* Myra Borchers for the Historic American Buildings Survey. *Courtesy:* Library of Congress 31

40. Wainwright Building, base. *Photo:* the author 32

41. Wainwright Building, east entrance. *Photo:* Lester Jones for the Historic American Buildings Survey. *Courtesy:* Library of Congress. 33

42. Wainwright Building, carved sandstone at south entrance. *Photo:* the author. 33

43. Wainwright Building, carved sandstone at east entrance. *Photo:* the author 33

44. Wainwright Building, doorplate and doorknob. *Photo:* Copyright © 1996, The Art Institute of Chicago; gift of Harry J. Scharres, 1973.738 a-b . . . 34

45. Wainwright Building, façade detail. *Photo:* Richard Nickel 34

46. Wainwright Building, view from Chestnut Street. *Photo:* Richard Nickel 35

47. Wainwright Building, typical bay, south front. *Diagram:* the author. 35

48. Wainwright Building, conjectural bay. *Diagram:* the author 36

49. Wainwright Building, attic detail. *Photo:* Richard Nickel 36

50. Wainwright Building, attic window, east front. *Photo:* the author 36

51. Wainwright Building. *Photo:* Richard Nickel 38

52. Wainwright Building, rendering. From *Engineering Magazine. Courtesy:* Linda Hall Library 39

53. Schiller Building and Borden Block, Chicago. *Photo:* Chicago Architectural Photo Company 39

54. Monadnock Block, Chicago, rendering. From the *Inland Architect. Courtesy:* The Art Institute of Chicago 40

55. Monadnock Block, east front. *Photo:* Richard Nickel 40

56. Reliance Building, Chicago. *Courtesy:* Gunny Harboe 41

57. Reliance Building, plan of corner pier and mullion. From J. K. Freitag, *Architectural Engineering* 42

58. Luxfer Prism project, façade. Copyright © 1998 The Frank Lloyd Wright Foundation. *Courtesy:* The Frank Lloyd Wright Archives 43

59. Larkin Building, Buffalo, N.Y. Adapted from *Ausgeführte Bauten und Entwürfe von Frank Lloyd Wright* . . 44

60. Larkin Building, plan above window sills. Adapted from *Ausgeführte Bauten und Entwürfe von Frank Lloyd Wright* 44

61. Larkin Building, light court. *Courtesy:* Buffalo and Erie County Historical Society 45

62. Unity Temple, Oak Park, Ill., rendering. Copyright © 1998 The Frank Lloyd Wright Foundation. *Courtesy:* The Frank Lloyd Wright Archives. 46

63. Unity Temple, interior. *Photo:* Chicago Architectural Photo Company. *Courtesy:* Art & Architecture Library, University of Michigan. 46

64. San Francisco *Call* project, perspective study. Copyright © 1998 The Frank Lloyd Wright Foundation. *Courtesy:* The Frank Lloyd Wright Archives. 47

65. San Francisco *Call* project, rendering. Copyright © 1998 The Frank Lloyd Wright Foundation. *Courtesy:* The Frank Lloyd Wright Archives. 47

66. Claus Spreckels Building, San Francisco. *Courtesy:* California Historical Society, San Francisco, Virginia M. Storti Collection. 49

67. Claus Spreckels Building, cantilever bracket. From J. K. Freitag, *Architectural Engineering.* 49

68. San Francisco project, floor plans. Copyright © 1998 The Frank Lloyd Wright Foundation. *Courtesy:* The Frank Lloyd Wright Archives. 50

69. Patented system for spandrels and cantilevered beltcourse, section and elevation. From E. L. Ransome and A. Saurbrey, *Reinforced Concrete Buildings.* 51

70. Model of San Francisco skyscraper project, on exhibit in 1914. *Courtesy:* The Frank Lloyd Wright Archives. 51

71. Play Mart project, Los Angeles, rendering. *Courtesy:* University Art Gallery, University of California–Santa Barbara 54

72. Skyscraper project, cross section. Copyright © 1998 The Frank Lloyd Wright Foundation 56

73. Skyscraper project, half-plan. Copyright © 1998 The Frank Lloyd Wright Foundation 57

74. National Life Insurance Company project, Chicago, rendering. Copyright © 1998 The Frank Lloyd Wright Foundation. *Courtesy:* The Frank Lloyd Wright Archives. 58

75. National Life Insurance Company project, aerial view. Copyright © 1998 The Frank Lloyd Wright Foundation. *Courtesy:* The Frank Lloyd Wright Archives. 59

76. National Life Insurance Company project, interior perspective. Copyright © 1998 The Frank Lloyd Wright Foundation. *Courtesy:* The Frank Lloyd Wright Archives. 60

77. National Life Insurance Company project, plan of twenty-second to twenty-fifth floors. Copyright © 1998 The Frank Lloyd Wright Foundation. *Courtesy:* The Frank Lloyd Wright Archives. 61

78. St. Mark's Tower project, New York, rendering. Copyright © 1998 The Frank Lloyd Wright Foundation. *Courtesy:* The Frank Lloyd Wright Archives. 62

79. Real estate map, St. Mark's neighborhood. Adapted from the *Manhattan Land Book. Courtesy:* New York City Landmarks Preservation Commission 65

80. St. Mark's Tower project, rendering of four towers. Copyright © 1998 The Frank Lloyd Wright Foundation. *Courtesy:* The Frank Lloyd Wright Archives. 66

81. St. Mark's Tower project, aerial perspective. Copyright © 1998 The Frank Lloyd Wright Foundation. *Courtesy:* The Frank Lloyd Wright Archives. 67

82. St. Mark's Tower project, plan. Copyright © 1998 The Frank Lloyd Wright Foundation. *Courtesy:* The Frank Lloyd Wright Archives 68

83. St. Mark's Tower project, elevation. Copyright © 1998 The Frank Lloyd Wright Foundation. *Courtesy:* The Frank Lloyd Wright Archives. 68

84. St. Mark's Tower project, cutaway perspective. Copyright © 1998 The Frank Lloyd Wright Foundation. *Courtesy:* The Frank Lloyd Wright Archives. 69

85. St. Mark's Tower project, cutaway perspective of bedroom mezzanine. Copyright © 1998 The Frank Lloyd Wright Foundation. *Courtesy:* The Frank Lloyd Wright Archives. 70

86. St. Mark's Tower project, section. Copyright © 1998 The Frank Lloyd Wright Foundation 70

87. Price Tower, Bartlesville, Okla., perspective study. Copyright © 1998 The Frank Lloyd Wright Foundation. *Courtesy:* The Frank Lloyd Wright Archives.   72

88. Price Tower, section through south side. Copyright © 1998 The Frank Lloyd Wright Foundation   73

89. Site preparation. *Photo:* Joe D. Price. *Courtesy:* Phillips Petroleum Company   73

90. Price Tower, rental plan. Copyright © 1998 The Frank Lloyd Wright Foundation   73

91. Price Tower, plan of bedroom mezzanine. Copyright © 1998 The Frank Lloyd Wright Foundation   74

92. Price Tower, elevator. *Photo:* Joe D. Price. *Courtesy:* Phillips Petroleum Company.   74

93. Price Tower, hall and entry to office. *Photo:* Joe D. Price. *Courtesy:* Phillips Petroleum Company   74

94. Price Tower, office quadrants and fire escape. *Photo:* Joe D. Price. *Courtesy:* Phillips Petroleum Company   75

95. Price Tower at night. *Photo:* Joe D. Price. *Courtesy:* Phillips Petroleum Company   76

96. Price Tower, office interior. *Photo:* Joe D. Price. *Courtesy:* Phillips Petroleum Company   77

97. Price Tower, living room. *Photo:* Joe D. Price. *Courtesy:* Phillips Petroleum Company   78

98. Price Tower, dining area. *Photo:* Joe D. Price. *Courtesy:* Phillips Petroleum Company   79

99. Price Tower, bedroom and balcony. *Photo:* Joe D. Price. *Courtesy:* Phillips Petroleum Company   80

100. Price Tower. *Photo:* Joe D. Price. *Courtesy:* Phillips Petroleum Company.   81

FRANK LLOYD WRIGHT, LOUIS SULLIVAN AND THE SKYSCRAPER

1. *Wainwright Building, St. Louis, looking northwest.*

INTRODUCTION

Louis Sullivan proclaimed himself the first architect to have discovered an authentically expressive form for the tall office building. This achievement, he said, came with the "very sudden and volcanic design" for the Wainwright Building, constructed in St. Louis in 1891–92 [Fig. 1]. Sullivan described the Wainwright Building as the birth of a "logical and poetic expression of the metallic frame construction." He compared it with the tulip that suddenly breaks into a gorgeous new variety. The modern skyscraper, he wrote, was meant to be a "unitary utterance, Dionysian in beauty" and "every inch a proud and soaring thing" [2].[1]

All of these statements are amazing because none of them is valid. Sullivan might have pretended to grasp the inner being of the tall office building, but he had dismissed as routine all the fundamental and defining factors in its construction. He chose to concern himself instead with emotional expression and a program for the metaphorical representation of what he took to be aspirant democracy and beneficent nature. Such intentions had nothing to do with a building type called forth by private speculation in commercial real estate. Skyscrapers were built not for sentiment and symbolism, but to make money. Costly to construct, they grew taller to superimpose more floors of office space for rent, not to celebrate a Dionysian vertical. The office spaces and structural bays in fact were disposed horizontally. Because office work called first of all for abundant daylight, light became the first principle of skyscraper architecture. Glass thus challenged all the traditions of the masonry wall Sullivan found so endearing.

Frank Lloyd Wright built his reputation with residential architecture and by a romantic accentuation of the horizontal in sympathy with an idea of the open landscape. At the same time, paradoxically, he grew to understand the skyscraper far better than did Sullivan. Wright could see that light should not only determine the logic of the tall office building but also inspire its poetics. Eventually, to secure the best light and air for a building-type traditionally urban, Wright envisioned skyscrapers scattered across the countryside as the beacons of small settlements. And he finally saw his only tall office tower constructed in a small city of the Middle West.

2. *Wainwright Building, east front.*

3

3. *Reliance Building, Chicago, main entrance.*

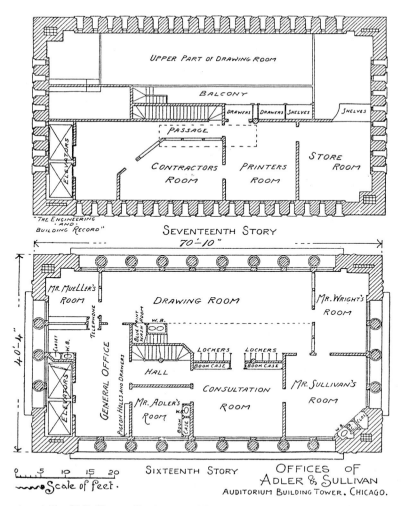

4. *Adler & Sullivan office layout, 1890.*

THE ENGINE OF PROFIT

In a tribute to Dankmar Adler, who had once been his partner, Louis Sullivan recalled that the men of Chicago "responsible for the modern office building" were William E. Hale and Owen F. Aldis. Neither, significantly, was an architect; both were engaged in commercial real estate. Hale began the Reliance Building, his most notable skyscraper, in 1890–91 by constructing its base beneath three stories of an old commercial block. When the rest of the old leases expired, four years later, he quickly added thirteen more stories. Such were the pressures of a real estate investment. An 1895 view of the main entrance to the Reliance Building leaves no doubt as to the purpose of a skyscraper [3].[1]

Sullivan often spoke plainly when he reminisced about Adler, because Adler attended to realities. Much about the partnership in fact could be inferred from the office layout [4]. Adler was the senior partner, but he had a room smaller than Sullivan's and smaller even than the corner office assigned to Frank Lloyd Wright, the chief draftsman. At the same time, Adler's location—next to the reception area, near the hall and the stairs to the contractors' room, and close to the office foreman, Paul Mueller—gave every sign that he was the partner who got things started and got them done. The plan sequestered Sullivan and left him free to pursue what he called a spontaneous "art of expression."[2]

Adler & Sullivan competed especially with the partnership of Burnham & Root, which enjoyed a large clientele that included both Hale and Aldis. Sullivan wrote in *The Autobiography of an Idea* that John Root had been an artist and Daniel Burnham a "colossal merchandiser." He nevertheless found that of the two, Burnham possessed the larger imagination:

> In each firm was a man with a fixed irrevocable purpose in life, for the sake of which he would bend or sacrifice all else. Daniel Burnham was obsessed by the feudal idea of power. Louis Sullivan was equally obsessed by the beneficent idea of Democratic power. Daniel chose the easier way, Louis the harder. Each brooded incessantly. John Root was so self-indulgent that there was risk he might never draw

upon his underlying power; Adler was essentially a technician, an engineer, a conscientious administrator, a large progressive judicial and judicious mind securing alike the confidence of conservative and radical, plenty of courage but lacking the dream-quality of Burnham; and such he must remain—the sturdy wheel-horse of a tandem team of which Louis did the prancing. Unquestionably, Adler lacked sufficient imagination; so in a way did John Root—that is to say, the imagination of the dreamer. In the dream-imagination lay Burnham's strength and Louis's passion.

Through his dream-imagination, Sullivan meant to redeem the skyscraper from "the speculator, the engineer, the builder." The artistic challenge of the tall office building, he said in 1896, was to proclaim from its dizzy height "the peaceful evangel of sentiment, of beauty, the cult of a higher life." Could any program have been more balmy? What was the virtue of a building that pretended to be something it was not?[3]

Untroubled by the dream-imagination, Adler concerned himself with the working drawings for a tall building, and how many man-hours it took to prepare them. He was not embarrassed to describe the Wainwright Building as "a plain business structure," because his vision of the skyscraper was nothing like Sullivan's:

> In a utilitarian age like ours it is safe to assume that the real-estate owner and the investor in buildings will continue to erect the class of buildings from which the greatest possible revenue can be obtained with the least possible outlay. . . . The purpose of erecting buildings other than those required for the shelter of their owners is specifically that of making investments for profit.

Adler found no reason to disguise the fact that the skyscraper was a business proposition intended to generate income from office space rented to business and professional people—in every sense, a bourgeois enterprise.[4]

Office buildings of any size were bought and sold much

like other investment vehicles. Late in 1890, about the time Sullivan designed the streetfronts of the Wainwright Building, commercial buildings came on the market in Chicago as so:

> Six-story office building on one of the best business corners of this city; well rented and susceptible of easy improvement and increased productiveness. Price $450,000.

> Six-story office building on a prominent corner near the Board of Trade. Pays over 6 per cent net. Price $200,000.

In St. Louis, where Chicago investors were said to be ready to construct a ten-story office building at Seventh and Olive streets, the price of the lot was reported to have risen over the years from $25,000 to $225,000. The *Post-Dispatch* commented that such an undertaking "by outside capitalists who have practical experience of the profits to be made out of the construction of large modern buildings in St. Louis, speaks volumes for the safety of such investments in this city."[5]

The rush to make a profit from a commercial building sometimes invited further risks. Burnham & Root's first large office building, the Grannis Block of 1880–81, famously burned on February 19, 1885, because at the eleventh hour of its construction so much wood was substituted for iron. Hence the Grannis Block "fell a victim to the Chicago vice of haste," Root remarked. It was meant to be fireproof, he said, "but there was a pressure to get it ready for the May rental, and the interior was finished in a hurry."[6]

In 1889, when the *Chicago Tribune* described the Tacoma Building, the Owings Building, and the new Chamber of Commerce Building as the "three most notable buildings now going up in Chicago," it also said they "must be viewed as nothing more nor less than huge money-making schemes." Because the purpose of the Tacoma Building was to create the largest amount of rentable space that a corner site of 80 by 100 feet could yield, the *Tribune* said, it made no effort toward architectural or picturesque effects: "It looks to be just what it is— a large collection of offices for the busy money-makers of Chicago."[7]

Even in the few tall buildings that embraced institutional functions and explicit symbolism—such as the Masonic Temple and the Woman's Temple, both designed by Burnham & Root—sentiment was "mixed with cold business policy," the *Tribune* noted [5]. They were expected to make money. Hence the spectacular Adler & Sullivan project of 1891 for an Odd Fellows'

Temple more than 550 feet tall was judged "possible from an architectural standpoint, but not probable from a financial point of view" [6]. In short:

> If there is one feature of Chicago's phenomenal business enterprise which receives general recognition it is her high buildings. The towering office building structures which have been erected during the last five years have brought the city prominently before the investing public all over the country.[8]

John Root, not so self-indulgent as Sullivan said, hoped to face the great engine of profit directly, as he told an architectural class at the Art Institute of Chicago in June 1890, only seven months before he died:

> How much "per cent" has always been considered foreign to art, and generally it is. Yet, curiously enough, it may sometimes guide art, if not positively

5. *Masonic Temple, Chicago, 1890–92. Demolished.*

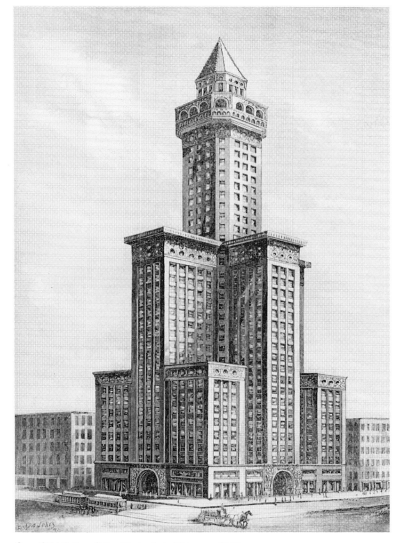

6.   *Odd Fellows' Temple project, Chicago, 1891.*

foster it. Art has never grown vitally without some sort of check, whether in the limitation of the age, the narrow yet intense idea which was the inspiration of the epoch, the specialized occupations of the moment, or some other equally valid cause . . . when a certain income must be derived by revenue from the building designed, every question must be carefully weighed, investigated in every possible light. . . .[9]

Sullivan wrote in 1896 that he meant to address the artistic problem of the tall office building by heeding the "imperative voice of emotion" and thus celebrating the "thrilling aspect" of loftiness; but, at the same moment, the historian A. D. F. Hamlin defined the new commercial structures as "buildings of excessive height." Barr Ferree, a critic who suggested that a "vertical system" was the most natural way to design a tall office building, nevertheless emphasized that the new architectural type, first and last, was "a commercial building, erected under commercial

impulses, answering to commercial needs, and fulfilling a commercial purpose in supplying its owner with a definite income." The tall building multiplied the original area of a city lot, Ferree said, by a dozen or more times. Tallness signified the desire for profit, not emotional exaltation:

> No architect designs a fourteen-story building because its height appeals to his artistic eye, or because he imagines it to be more artistic in appearance than a ten-story one.

Yet such was the illogic of Sullivan's rhetoric that he proposed to make the tall office building not only a "proud and soaring thing" but an "eloquent peroration of most bald, most sinister, most forbidding conditions."[10]

Sullivan pronounced every building past or present a "social act," and in his *Kindergarten Chats* urged an imaginary postgraduate student "to look upon architecture not merely as an art more or less well, more or less badly, done, but as a social manifestation." But in his essay of 1896 on the tall building he put aside the "social conditions" to avoid the fact that the social problem was not that of expressing what he deemed the "force and power of altitude" in the skyscraper but of *reducing* its awesome presence and overwhelming scale.[11]

Even in 1866, before skyscrapers had appeared, Frederick Law Olmsted declared his opposition to "lofty and compact buildings" unless crowding and the "consideration of ground-rent" clearly overruled "considerations of taste and convenience of use." Nearly twenty years later, the English architect Robert Kerr wrote that the balance sheet for the tall buildings of New York presented "nothing but a ground-rent" on one side and on the other "any number of considerations of *scale*":

> Physically we are what we are, however grand may be our aspirations; our home is on the ground, and neither in the trees nor in the clouds. . . . Americans are no doubt accustomed to large ideas; I have said all my life that no one can appreciate true freedom of mind who has not seen the Americans at home; but when we hear of warehouses and dwelling-houses, even in America, attaining a height of one hundred and sixty feet from the level of the ground, while men and women, even in America, are still only from five and a half to six feet high, the inquiry is surely a reasonable one whether the houses are not a little too tall for the people.[12]

Was the citizen at street level expected to be grateful for the immense size and height of buildings intended to generate private profit? There were more urgent social concerns: the threat of fires, collapse from earthquakes or structural fatigue and failure; the loss of light to neighboring buildings and for street life; traffic congestion; and the complexities and increased costs of utilities and sanitation. Much like the "social evil"—prostitution—the tall office building could easily be perceived as a menace, an urban malady.

Sullivan in 1891 had considered the claims of public welfare against those of private property. He noted that the individual owner sought rentable space while the public demanded light and air:

> It seems to me a subject not at all debatable that here in Chicago the freedom of thought and action of the individual should be not only maintained, but held sacred. By this I surely do not mean the license of the individual to trample on his neighbor and disregard the public welfare, but I do just as surely mean that our city has acquired and maintained its greatness by virtue of its brainy men, who have made it what it is and who guarantee its future. These men may be selfish enough to need regulation, but it is monstrous to suppose that they must be suppressed, for they have in themselves qualities as noble, daring, and inspired as ever quickened knights of old to deeds of chivalry.

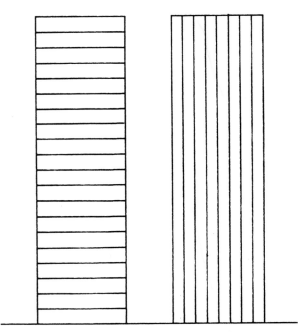

8. *Skyscraper expression, horizontal vs. vertical.*

7. *Street view of conjectural setback skyscrapers, 1891.*

Sullivan suggested a strict rule of progressive setbacks in the upper stories of tall buildings. But his dream-imagination conjured gigantic structures and a center that reduced the citizenry to the scale of insects, a place as aesthetically chaotic as the laissez-faire American city had already become [7].[13]

A skyscraper city that so accommodated the chivalrous men of real-estate speculation might easily be seen as a Babel, even a necropolis, and it often was. Paradoxically, moreover, the function of the tall office building, as Robert Kerr observed in 1884, was to rent space horizontally disposed. Sullivan admitted that the skyscraper was largely "an indefinite number of stories of offices piled tier upon tier," just as Paul Bourget, the French novelist and critic, reported after a visit to Chicago that its architects "ruthlessly accepted the speculator's inspired conditions,—to multiply as much as possible the value of the bit of earth at the base by multiplying the superimposed 'offices.' . . ."[14]

Hence a forthright, logical exposition of the skyscraper would have expressed the superimposed floors, the insistent reiteration of the horizontal [8]. Sullivan's ecstasy of the vertical stood diametrically opposite the nature of the tall office building. The "final, comprehensive formula" he proposed in 1896 as a solution to the artistic problem of the skyscraper in fact suppressed what related most of all to human scale and daily office work: the floor levels. He merely forecast tall buildings that would appear extruded, not constructed.[15]

THE GREAT DESIDERATUM

Because skyscrapers were built to create space for rent, they needed first of all to provide plentiful daylight for the conduct of office work. The new building type thus addressed in a special way the fundamental paradox of architecture, that in this most substantial of the visual arts the essential constituents—space and light—are intangible and indeed invisible.[1]

In 1884, after he had reviewed four alternative plans by Burnham & Root for a tall office building in Chicago, the Boston investor Peter C. Brooks summed up the situation in only five words: "Light is the great desideratum." He echoed Frederick Baumann, a Chicago architect who in that year published a penetrating theory for improving the construction of tall buildings. Baumann may have had the habit of laughing "like a goat," as Sullivan wrote, but he was no one's fool; even Sullivan, who once worked in his office, granted that he was "most illuminating, bare of delusion." In a symposium of 1887 he emphasized utility as the true basis of the architectural art. Baumann also quoted from the German architect Gottfried Semper: "Style is the coincidence of a structure with the conditions of its origin." But he was best known for a treatise he published in 1873 under the cumbrous title of *The Art of Preparing Foundations for All Kinds of Buildings, with Particular Illustration of the "Method of Isolated Piers" as Followed in Chicago.* Many years later, Dankmar Adler called it a classic text and said that Baumann's presentation was masterly and lucid. Sullivan, however, made the mistake of regarding Baumann as the "master of one idea," for Baumann's paper on foundations paled in comparison to his overall conception of the tall building.[2]

Baumann's theory for improving the skyscraper first appeared in March 1884, when an obscure journal named *The Sanitary News* reported his idea was to erect "a firm and rigid skeleton, or hull, of iron, and cover it at once with a proper roof." The iron uprights were to carry the enclosing veneer of stone, terra cotta, or brick:

> Mr. Baumann claims that this method would render the work more independent of the weather than by the usual construction; the erection of the iron hull is, in its nature, a rapid process. The practicability of erecting buildings on Chicago soil, twelve and more stories high, then becomes a fact. Light, the great desideratum in all city buildings, is secured. . . .[3]

Baumann published his pamphlet on *Improvement in the Construction of Tall Buildings* in December 1884:

> Occupants seek convenience, *secureness* and *light*; all this, of course, combined with a shine of elegance.
>
> The highest success in a happy combination of these four points will lead to the highest possible and most permanent rental. . . .
>
> LIGHT—the most indispensable desideratum with a building is procured even in the lowest, most valuable, stories, where otherwise the necessarily broad piers would be a hinderment.
>
> The piers may not only be made narrow, but shallow also—27 inches at the most—and this, again, is a saving of light.
>
> The iron uprights are to be provided with a series of projecting brackets for the purpose of anchoring and *supporting* the parts forming the exterior enclosure.

In the construction of buildings, Baumann concluded, the four most important considerations were "*Light, Convenience, Space, Time.*" He understood perfectly the rise of the skyscraper.[4]

The function of what Sullivan called the metallic frame construction was neither aesthetic nor philosophic, but entirely economic. Like so many other technological advances of the day—improvements in the passenger elevator, fireproofing, foundations, windbracing, ventilation, plumbing, and heating—the metal skeleton gave rise to the tall office building only in the sense that it became an enabling factor. In Aristotle's terms, it was neither the formal nor final cause. Purpose inspired the technology, and the purpose of the skyscraper was to generate profits. "Tall buildings will pay well in Chicago hereafter," Peter C. Brooks wrote Owen Aldis on March 22, 1881, "and sooner or later a way will be found to erect them."[5]

By 1895 the engineer Corydon T. Purdy already could

look back on the development of the skyscraper and confess that the "remarkable enterprise of Chicago has made such great demands upon both architects and engineers that they have been forced to be progressive." In the evolution of the steel frame, he said, the most notably progressive architects had been William Le Baron Jenney, Burnham & Root, and Holabird & Roche. Chicago channeled its remarkable enterprise into commercial real estate, which demanded the great desideratum, light. Or, as Jenney noted in October 1885:

> As it was important in the Home Insurance Building [at the northeast corner of La Salle and Adams streets] to obtain a large number of small offices with abundance of light, the piers between the windows were reduced to the minimum, and the following system of construction was adopted.
>
> Iron was used as the skeleton of the entire building except the party walls, and every piece of iron was protected from fire by masonry, excepting only some columns so situated as not to be dangerous if left exposed.[6]

A few years later, Jenney again discussed the "Chicago construction":

> In 1884 the Home Insurance company of New York built the first tall fire-proof, finely-finished office building erected in Chicago. It demanded the maximum amount of light, reducing the piers and wall to dimensions that forced the architect [Jenney] to adopt a new method of construction that has since been generally adopted and is now known as the Chicago construction.
>
> This construction carries all the loads on metal columns which are placed in the piers and in the walls. They not only carry the floor girders, but also the entire walls, story by story, by means of beams or lintels from column to column. . . . The masonry is reduced on the exterior to what is necessary to hold the window frames and to fireproof the metal. . . . The same science, and the same superintendence, is required in calculating and erecting one of these high buildings as in a steel railroad bridge of the first order.[7]

Sullivan had also worked for Jenney, whom he condescended to recall as a bon vivant and raconteur, "a free-and-easy cultured gentleman, but not an architect except by courtesy of terms." But it was in Jenney's office that he had met John Edelmann, whose theory of suppressed

9. *Leiter Building, Chicago, detail of east face. Demolished.*

functions illuminated the "final, comprehensive formula" that Sullivan so eagerly applied to all aspects of art and life. He might have chosen instead to pay better attention to Jenney and Baumann, and especially to the rational way in which Jenney delineated the windows and walls of the exemplary Leiter Building of 1879, at the northwest corner of Wells and Monroe streets [9]. With floor girders connected to iron columns at the inner faces of the piers, the five-story building came close to being skeletal. The bays measured 24 feet 8½ inches wide and accommodated three window openings, each 6 feet 5½ inches wide. Constructed simply as a warehouse and store building, not for offices and desk work, the Leiter Building nevertheless admitted a generous amount of light.[8]

Even an architect of little renown could demonstrate an understanding of the tall commercial building that surpassed Sullivan's. As the wholesale district of Chicago shifted southward, Charles L. Willoughby, who ran two clothing stores, decided to construct a building "for traveling men's sample rooms" at the northwest corner of Franklin and Jackson streets. Late in 1887, George H. Edbrooke designed for him a spidery nine-story structure

11.   *Marshall Field Wholesale Store, Chicago, looking southwest. Demolished.*

10.   *Willoughby Building, Chicago, detail of south front. Demolished.*

with iron and glass streetfronts [10]. Significantly, the huge wholesale store that H. H. Richardson designed for Marshall Field stood only half a block away [11]. It too was new, and it was the building Sullivan chose to celebrate in the *Kindergarten Chats* as an oasis, an elemental outburst of form in a world of "barren pettiness." The oasis nevertheless represented an ancient way of building in monumental fronts of stone, a tradition its slight and modest neighbor left behind, and thus declared irrelevant. The future belonged to the Willoughby Building and its great plate-glass windows, which nearly met [12]. If it was true, as Sullivan said, that "every problem contains and suggests its own solution," the answer to the challenge of the tall building was an architecture of glass, not mass.[9]

Oddly enough, glass already had conquered the masonry wall in countless commercial buildings constructed with cast-iron fronts. Some proved amazingly light and airy. A. T. Stewart liked to compare the white fronts of his Uptown Store on Broadway at Tenth Street in New York to puffs of white clouds rising high above the sidewalk [13]. The idea of the cast-iron front had been implicit in the framing of mill buildings near the end of the eighteenth century, and the advance to a metal skeleton might seem to have been obvious as the next step. But cast-iron

12.   *Willoughby Building, interior.*

13.   *A. T. Stewart Store, New York, east front. Demolished.*

columns fell from favor, except in New York. Unlike members of steel, they could not bend, and in fires they broke suddenly and completely. Taste turned more conservative, preferring building fronts that looked substantial and reassuring. Richardson's masterly performances in brick and stone grew exceedingly popular.[10]

Most early skyscrapers embodied the conflict between a nostalgia for masonry walls and the new logic of skeletal construction in the service of light. A tall structure so conspicuously incoherent as the Fagin Building in St. Louis might indeed be ridiculed, as when the *Architectural Record* declared it "so far as we know . . . the most discreditable piece of architecture in the United States." It faced north on Olive Street between Eighth and Ninth streets and bristled with projecting bays of glass designed to catch the light [14]. But the writer who dismissed the front of the Fagin Building as "nothing but a sash-frame" merely displayed his ignorance of the great desideratum.[11]

Just as light ruled the logic of the tall office building, it suggested a more appropriate aesthetic. Burnham & Root were to discern this very early; their familiar Rookery of 1885–88, a surprisingly genial office building at the southeast corner of La Salle and Adams streets in Chicago, gained its commodious plan from a site large enough for a central light court, which they vaulted with a grand skylight [15, 16]. Details such as the perforated girders, per-

14. *Fagin Building, St. Louis. Demolished.*

15. *The Rookery, Chicago, light court, looking southwest.*

16.   *The Rookery, light court, looking east.*

forated stair risers, openwork-metal arabesques, and ornamental flourishes painted in gold and white were all
inspired by a close attention to the blessings of light.[12]

But the one building of 1880s Chicago that testified
most immediately to the need for light was the Tacoma
Building, constructed in 1888–89 two blocks north of the
Rookery, at the northeast corner of La Salle and Madison
streets [17]. Holabird & Roche, its architects, had been
approached a few years earlier by Wirt D. Walker, who like
Owen Aldis was a lawyer engaged in commercial real
estate. Walker held a site only 25 feet deep but with a
frontage of 100 feet on Madison Street. The *Chicago
Tribune* reported in January 1888 that he was planning "an
expensive store and office building" on the narrow plot.
"The office portion of the building promises to meet with
equal popularity [to that of the storefronts]," the paper
said, "as every office is a front one and has south light."[13]

Walker soon enlarged the site to an 80-foot front on La
Salle Street, and in March 1888 the *Tribune* again took
note:

The plans . . . are not yet complete, but there is no
doubt that the structure will be one of the finest in
the city. A careful study has been made of the question how to get the most light with the least sacrifice
of space. . . .

The final plan illustrated how aggressively light could be
pursued [18]. Two projecting bays comprising eight windows formed the salient and greatly enhanced the prestige of the broad corner offices. The insistent projecting
bays, intended to expand the space for rent, gave the
building a strangely embattled appearance. Shortly after
it opened on May 1, 1889, the building was described by
the anonymous Chicago correspondent of the *American
Architect and Building News*:

The construction of the two fronts is that of the iron
column covered with masonry that has been so fre-
quently used in Chicago, although in this case it
would seem as if it had been reduced to its last
expression. . . .

17. *Tacoma Building, Chicago. Demolished.*

At the end of 1889, Henry Van Brunt, a literate and conservative architect who had moved from Boston to Kansas City, Missouri, wrote that the commercial architecture of the West showed "a greater freedom from the restraints of the European schools" than that of the East. Van Brunt accurately defined the great desideratum:

> No accepted formulas are permitted to interfere with the primary necessity of abundant interior light. The first consideration is that windows shall be large enough and frequent enough for this exacting service, without regard to any studio predilections, furnished by the noble wall surfaces of Italian palaces and medieval monasteries, or by any of the buttressed or pilastered symmetries of the Old World.

John Root, in his paper on "A Great Architectural Problem," also emphasized the primacy of daylight:

> Of course, the first radical question to suggest itself is that of light. . . . Experience has demonstrated that all spaces within the enclosure of four walls which are not well lighted by sunshine, or at least direct daylight, are in office buildings non-productive. The elementary question, therefore, is how to so arrange the building upon its lot that every foot within it shall be perfectly lighted. . . . To ascertain this it is necessary to know by experiment to what depth

Built avowedly as a money-making scheme, and every consideration of looks made entirely subservient to that of utility, it is only to be wondered that the exterior looks as well as it does. It is exactly what it purports to be—straightforward construction repeated story after story. . . .[14]

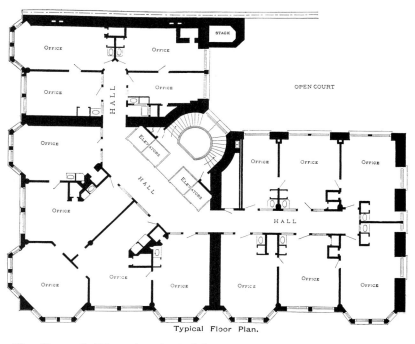

18. *Tacoma Building, plan of typical floor.*

from the front wall daylight will reach, upon the average, in a story of convenient height, and giving to the space to be lighted the largest possible windows.[15]

Tall office buildings until the 1940s largely depended on natural light. In 1892, when Dankmar Adler wrote about the critical need for a "sufficient volume of daylight for purposes of reading and writing," he barely mentioned artificial light:

> I cannot agree with those who place the matter of structural design as first in importance. I can easily imagine a tall office building most admirable in everything that relates to mere construction, and yet worthless to its owners.
>
> The first requisite to the successful operation of any premises for use as offices by professional and business men is light and air.

The experience of real-estate agents shows that high rentals can be obtained only for well-lighted offices, and that the most desirable tenants will not occupy inferior or ill-lighted rooms at ever so low a rental.[16]

Louis Sullivan chose a different path. Many years later, curiously, he wrote that in his early years with Adler the "immediate problem was increased daylight, the maximum of daylight." For that reason, they narrowed the piers and favored the windows. Sullivan nevertheless preferred to see in the slender piers "the beginnings of a vertical system." Preoccupied with emotional release and his personal symbolic program, he gave the piers the aesthetic and metaphorical task of transforming the tall office building into a monumental presence "rising from the earth as a unitary utterance, Dionysian in beauty." He confused means with ends, and he lost sight of the great desideratum.[17]

SULLIVAN'S DREAM

Because he believed the dream-imagination could carry his art into a higher realm, Sullivan discounted the basic facts of the skyscraper and even his own occasional ability to recognize them. His predisposition to high-minded and often foggy thought became obvious early on. In 1882 a reporter for the *Inter Ocean* had tried to interview him about a design for a theater:

> Mr. Sullivan is a pleasant gentleman, but somewhat troubled with large ideas tending to metaphysics. . . . It is therefore difficult to learn from Mr. Sullivan just what he has done. He refers to that work you will see about the stage opening as the differentiation of an absolute truth having something to do with Spencer's first principles and Darwin's doctrine of evolution, with the predicate of a flower and an ordinary staircase for an hypothesis.

A few years later, Sullivan bewildered a convention of architects by musing at length about inspiration and its relation to nature's rhythms of growth and decay:

> Effusing from such wonders interblended all around, has come to me thus, in soft pulsations, the elemental voice of Nature yearning. Whereby deeply do I know, thou generous and kindly Springtime, why I was touched, O, Prodigal! and captivated by thy presence. Now, nevermore to cease in its crescendo, has the lark's refrain returned in part to thee, a rhapsody of echoes from my soul.

Patter so sentimental as that helped explain how Sullivan came to think the tall office building expressed a romantic impulse to build skyward and best served as an icon of the forthcoming brotherhood of democratic man. His fellow architects knew better. So, at times, did he.[1]

For he also praised the business energies of the Midwest in order to admonish his colleagues that their "ability to develop elementary ideas organically" was far from conspicuous:

> In this respect, the architect is inferior to the businessman and financier, whose capacity to expand a simple, congenial idea, once fixed, into subtle, manifold and consistent ramifications is admirable. . . .

In later years, moreover, he recalled that the pressures that made Chicago into a great center had been overwhelmingly economic:

> Thus the year 1880 may be set as the zero hour of an amazing expansion, for by that time the city had recovered from the shock of the panic of 1873. Manufacturing expanded with incredible rapidity, and the building industry took on an organizing definition. With the advance in land values, and a growing sense of financial stability, investors awakened to opportunity, and speculators and promoters were at high feast. The tendency in commercial buildings was toward increasing stability, durability, and height. . . .

Sullivan found 1880 to be the zero hour of his own career, as well; he and Adler took such care in constructing the Borden Block, he recalled, that "the building was rented six weeks before it was finished and it did us much good professionally."[2]

Yet he refused to see himself as a servant of the business world or, more specifically, of the surge in real estate speculation. His own program for a building blithely diverged from the client's, as if fully entitled to exist separately. He intended to reach far beyond the concerns of architecture. In opposition to Ruskin's observation that "sculpture is the representation of an idea, while architecture is itself a real thing," Sullivan thought of a building primarily as an opportunity for poetic metaphor.[3]

A careful reading of his essay of 1896 on the tall office building merely proved how irrational the dream-imagination could become. Sullivan deplored the new building type as "this sterile pile, this crude, harsh, brutal agglomeration," cited its mundane facts and conditions, then hailed the "imperative voice of emotion" and the thrill of verticality. Through that astonishing reversal, the "sinister building" not only became a "proud and soaring thing" but "one of the most stupendous, one of the most magnificent opportunities that the Lord of Nature in His beneficence has ever offered to the proud spirit of man."[4]

Sullivan's art of expression, as he called it, thus gloried in a gratuitous claim to spiritual meanings that by no means inhered in the tall office building. In a further confusion, he professed to have fathomed the hidden character of "function." He told of the epiphany he had experienced while listening to John Edelmann:

> One day John explained his theory of *suppressed functions*; and Louis, startled, saw in a flash that this meant the real clue to the mystery that lay behind the veil of appearances. Louis was peculiarly subject to shock from [the] unexpected explosion of a single word; and when the word "function" was detonated by the word "suppressed," a new, an immense idea came suddenly into being and lit up his inner and his outer world as one.[5]

The immense idea became in Sullivan's mind a law, as he repeated nine times in his essay on the tall office building, and a "final, comprehensive formula." This he now stated as "form ever follows function," a dictum he proposed to apply to the skyscraper:

> Shall we, then, daily violate this law in our art? . . . Is it indeed a truth so transparent that we see through it but do not see it? Is it really, then, a very marvelous thing, or is it rather so commonplace, so everyday, so near a thing to us, that we cannot perceive that the shape, form, outward expression, design or whatever we may choose, of the tall office building should in the very nature of things follow the functions of the building? . . .

When he reminisced about the zero-hour of his career, Sullivan simplified the law into "form follows function":

> He could now, undisturbed, start on the course of practical experimentation he long had in mind, which was to make an architecture that fitted its functions—a realistic architecture based on well defined utilitarian needs—that all practical demands of utility should be paramount as basis of planning and design; that no architectural dictum, or tradition, or superstition, or habit, should stand in the way.[6]

But if the real purpose of the skyscraper was to produce income from an investment, the building needed first of all to serve the practical demands of the tenants. The paramount conditions of planning and design were precisely those that Sullivan found mundane, thus consigned to Adler as having to do strictly with the economics of the building. "I assume them to have been fully considered and disposed of," he wrote, "to the satisfaction of purely utilitarian and pecuniary demands."[7]

The dream-imagination proposed instead to transform the tall office building into a subjective and spiritual undertaking by changing its "function" into a blend of emotional expression with symbolic representation. By the mere "addition of a certain quality and quantity of sentiment," Sullivan hoped, the commercial nature of the skyscraper could be transcended. His own interests might well have existed independently of architecture.[8]

In the pronouncements of his later years the function of the dream-imagination grew ever more perplexing. The world of American business, which he had often dismissed but occasionally praised, Sullivan now condemned as vicious:

> Look at your business. What is it become but a war of extermination among cannibals? Does it express Democracy? . . . How glibly have you acquiesced! With what awful folly have you assumed selfish egotism to be the basis of Democracy! . . . And, to end with, you are old enough, and have found the time to succeed in nearly making a fine art of—Betrayal, and a science of—Graft!

All this begged the question of how the skyscraper was to become a spiritual expression.[9]

Every building stood as a social act, Sullivan said; by social act, however, he meant "the nature of the thoughts of the individual and the people whose image the building is or was." Architecture thus defined could never be more than a metaphor of something else, the spirit of the times. Hence the irony of Sullivan's protest against a facile use of the historic styles when he himself proposed a more insidious historicism. Buildings conceived as symbolic expressions of the Zeitgeist merely contrived to address the future by attempting to create what would then document the past.[10]

A national architecture attained perfection, Ruskin said, by becoming memorial or monumental; its first duty was to "render the architecture of the day historical." But a building conceived to represent history could too conveniently deny what Ruskin described as the "restless and discontented present." The young American historian Frederick Jackson Turner, by contrast, welcomed the present and disdained the architectural monuments of the past for having arisen from the woes of the common people. "Our times," he wrote approvingly, "are plebeian; it is visible in our architecture." Sullivan thought his mission was to interpret the life of the American people, but in the plebeian architecture of his restless and discontented time he saw only a rapacious and "feudal" stage of capitalism. Hence he aimed to prove himself "a democratic citizen, not a lackey, a true exponent of democracy, not a tool . . . of anarchy."[11]

America settled a new and spacious land to serve the "world-spirit" of democracy, Sullivan wrote. Thus the deeply tainted democracy of "raging materialism" and a "money-crazy people" was impeding the aspirant democracy of beneficent power, universal love, the brotherhood of man, and the "altruistic activity of the Ego."[12]

Sullivan set out to redeem the skyscraper from the "most bald, most sinister, most forbidding conditions" by changing it into a symbol of "the cult of a higher life." His program called for nothing less than a regeneration of democracy and of man himself. Such a grandiose project for the tall office building can only seem incredible; but he also intended to make the building a metaphor of the exuberance and bounty of nature. For if democracy arose as history's purpose for America in the unfolding of the "world-spirit," it also presented nature's plan for man:

> We live under a form of government called Democracy. And we, the people of the United States of America, constitute the most colossal instance known in history of a people seeking to verify the fundamental truth that self-government is Nature's law for Man.[13]

By his faith in an architecture conceived as a "glowing and gloriously wrought metaphor" of aspirant democracy and beneficent nature, Sullivan shifted again the meaning of "function." Now the purpose of the tall office building was to "arrest and typify in materials the harmoniously interblended rhythms of nature and humanity." Sullivan posited "a certain function, aspirant democracy" that sought a certain form of expression, democratic architecture. Because he had redefined "function" as an originating pressure or impulse, he could believe that an architecture of metaphor answered to his law that form follows function. The "outburst of form" expressed by the Dionysian verticals of the tall office building would thus signify the aspirant impulse, or "the urge of Democracy and a luxuriantly vital continent":

> . . . the spirit of democracy is a function seeking expression in organized social form. I have stated also that every function is a subdivision or phase of that energy which we have called the Infinite Creative Spirit and which we may now call the Function of all functions.

By trying to embody this high-flown rhetoric of utopian democracy (the "primordial world-aspiration") and beneficent nature (the "one unfailing source, the visible effect of creative energy"), Sullivan merely diminished the building art to streetfronts, to oversized and occult emblems.[14]

19.   *Wainwright Building, south front.*

THE WAINWRIGHT BUILDING

Louis Sullivan considered the Wainwright Building the great turning point of his career [19]. Other buildings qualified as favorites, but none contested the importance he assigned to the Wainwright Building:

> As to my buildings: Those that interest me date from the Wainwright Bldg. in St. Louis. . . . The Prudential Bldg. [in Buffalo, New York] is the "sister" of the Wainwright. All my commercial buildings since the Wainwright are conceived in the same general spirit. . . . The structures prior to the Wainwright were in my "masonry" period. The Auditorium Bldg. and Walker Bldg., Chicago, are the best of the large ones—the Ryerson, Getty, and Wainwright tombs, among the small.[1]

In no true sense could the Wainwright Building claim a civic or public purpose. Built as an engine of profit, it generated monthly dividends in 1925 at the rate of 8.4 percent a year. In 1940, as the building approached fifty years old, its capitalization was reduced from $700,000 to $385,000, and on that basis its yield in 1946 came to more than 11 percent.[2]

Nothing about the origins of the Wainwright Building testified to an urge for emotional expression—or validated a program of metaphorical representation. St. Louis by 1890 had become the fourth largest city in the country, surpassed only by New York, Chicago, and Philadelphia, and its surprising growth encouraged rampant speculation in real estate. When the *Republic* reported on May 30, 1890, that a downtown corner lot was sold to an unidentified party, it also noted a "fair share of competition over the deal" and the next day described the transaction as "personal speculation in view of the rapid development of property in the central part of town." The sale of a consortium of local breweries to an English syndicate had generated a large pool of capital for real-estate speculation, said both the *Globe-Democrat* and the *Post-Dispatch*. It was soon rumored that the president of the St. Louis Brewing Association, Ellis Wainwright, had bought the site in question. On June 1 the *Republic* said an eight-story office building would be constructed at a cost of $500,000:

> Although Mr. Wainwright bought the property on speculation he wisely changed his mind, as he will doubtless find it to his advantage to expend the sum named in erecting such a huge building. . . . Several prominent real estate dealers will occupy offices in the building.[3]

But in fact Catherine D. Wainwright, his mother, bought the site and became the majority shareholder in the building company. She was then sixty-four; later, in a biographical sketch of her husband, Samuel Wainwright, she was described as a woman "of exceptional force of character and excellent business ability." (After her death on October 10, 1900, the *Globe-Democrat* noted both that she was wealthy and that she had been one of the largest realty holders in the city. "One of the monuments to her judgment," the paper said, "is the Wainwright office building.") Mrs. Wainwright paid $127,000 for the site at the northwest corner of Seventh and Chestnut streets. Daniel Catlin, the seller, had paid only $90,000 for the same property eight months earlier when he bought it from the notorious New York financier Jay Gould, fair testimony to the fever of real estate speculation in St. Louis.[4]

Gould held the property from April 1887 until late in September 1889, but realized a profit of only $7,000—a fact that pleased the *Globe-Democrat,* which noted "his great bluff toward the erection of a magnificent railway office building." Earlier, the site had been occupied by six three-story brick buildings on Chestnut Street and a pair of two-story buildings on Seventh Street; Gould demolished the old buildings to make way for the office block he never built. Hence the *Globe-Democrat* reported on June 5, 1890, that Wainwright and his mother would rescue an unsightly lot:

> It seems certain now that the Seventh and Chestnut street vacant corner will contain improvements other than the bill boards which have adorned the site during the last few years. . . . The proposed structure will be ten stories in height. . . . When completed the structure will be known as the Wainwright building, to be owned jointly by Mr. Wainwright and his mother.[5]

Even before Mrs. Wainwright took title to the property, the *Post-Dispatch* remarked upon the primary importance of light. The proposed office building, the newspaper said, promised to be "the most perfectly naturally lighted building in the city." It would benefit from two streetfronts, the paper said, and from the alleys at the other elevations, and would use "all the plate glass possible consistent with strength." In the months to come, a concern for strength—and especially the *appearance* of strength—would oppose the great desideratum.[6]

The newspapers did not mention an architect; nor did the building process get under way. Months passed by. Ellis Wainwright, who turned forty that summer, sailed for Europe. His absence seemed not to affect the plans for the office building, as the *Post-Dispatch* reported on September 18, 1890:

> Ellis Wainwright will commence putting up one of the finest office buildings in the city as soon as he returns from Europe. Plans for this improvement are ready and have been submitted.[7]

Submitted by whom? And to whom? Who provided that information? If it was Catherine Wainwright, how far did she proceed while Ellis Wainwright was in Europe? On November 7, 1890, the *Globe-Democrat* published a small and clumsy engraving based on "designs by Charles K. Ramsey," a St. Louis architect [20]. It depicted the Wainwright Building as a nine-story structure characterized by broad corner piers and arcading at the sixth story. The windows were paired, with most of them subsumed by the arcades. The entrance on Chestnut Street featured a Romanesque arch, or what the newspaper described as "a granite archway 14 feet high and a vestibule 14 feet wide." Once again the project was praised for attending to light. "The use of an abundance of plate glass, giving outside light to every office," the *Globe-Democrat* said, "makes it particularly desirable."[8]

But when did Ramsey associate with Adler & Sullivan? And why? Did the little engraving represent Ramsey's conception or an early scheme Sullivan had sent him? Many questions remain unanswered, but in any event the "very sudden and volcanic design" in truth represented Sullivan's revision of an earlier design. He changed the streetfronts by eliminating the sixth-story arcade and the arch at the entrance. Yet if his purpose, as John Edelmann implied, was to make certain that "the rectangular steel skeleton is expressed in rectangular outer forms," why, in later skyscraper designs, did he revert to arcading and the arch?[9]

If the commission originally was Ramsey's, and Adler &

20. *Wainwright Building, preliminary scheme.*

Sullivan entered the picture rather late in the day to redesign the façades and prepare the working drawings, why did the Chicago architects always take precedence in the credits? Or did the *Globe-Democrat* simply fail to report that Adler & Sullivan were involved early on? Could it be that Ramsey avoided any mention of Sullivan in order to inflate his own role? After all, he had once gained national attention in a most embarrassing way, when the *American Architect and Building News,* of Boston, commented:

> We think it useful to give due publicity to the enterprise of Messrs. Raeder & Ramsey, architects, of St. Louis (or of Mr. Charles K. Ramsey, who seems to have succeeded this firm). These practitioners have adopted an advertising expedient not without ingenuity in its conception and doubtless satisfactory in its pecuniary results. They have published an "Architectural Guide" for gratuitous circulation. . . . We conceive that the circulation of this book was intended to be confined to the far West, because among the illustrations we discover over the unblushing legend, "Raeder & Ramsey, architects," the design of the Shillaber Building on Court Street

in Boston. . . . We do not suppose that Messrs. Cummings & Sears, the architects of this building, will be inclined to take any action with regard to this, but in the interest of common decency and honor in the practice of the profession, we cannot suffer it to pass by without an appreciative notice. . . .[10]

Ramsey was a native of Godfrey, Illinois. Raised in St. Louis, where his father became a prominent building contractor, he was sent to study in Paris, and he traveled in Europe only a few years before Sullivan studied at the Ecole des Beaux Arts. Ramsey returned to St. Louis to begin his practice, and the incident of the "Architectural Guide" seems not to have damaged his reputation for long. When the Western Association of Architects was organized in November 1884 in Chicago, he was named chairman of the committee on bylaws. Sullivan and Ramsey both took part in discussions at the convention, as they would again the next year at a convention in St. Louis. Upon the organization of the St. Louis chapter of the American Institute of Architects, in 1890, Ramsey was elected its treasurer.

As for Ramsey's practice, the Houser Building of 1888–89 could serve as characteristic [21]. It stood at the northwest corner of Broadway and Chestnut Street, only two blocks east of the Wainwright site. The design drew upon the Insurance Exchange of 1884–85 and the Phenix Building of 1885–87, two of Burnham & Root's tall buildings in Chicago.[11]

The *Post-Dispatch* of November 7, 1890, repeated what the *Globe-Democrat* had published that morning and confirmed that the excavation for the Wainwright Building was under way. Again there was no mention of Adler & Sullivan; and except for a few dimensions, the plan already could be described virtually as it would be executed:

> To obtain the greatest amount of light and ventilation with little waste of space as possible the architect has arranged the ground plan of the building very much in the form of a double **L**. This plan provides for a court opening to the north 32 feet wide and having a depth of 65 feet, that is, extending into the building within 49 feet of the Chestnut street front. To still further facilitate light and ventilation in the rear, there is a 9-foot offset on the west side of the building, commencing 49 feet from the Chestnut street front. This arrangement gives a light shaft 24 feet wide, with the alley, for offices in the northwestern section of the building. . . .

On November 11 the city issued a permit to "erect foun-

21. *Houser Building, St. Louis. Demolished.*

dation for a brick office building" at the northwest corner of Seventh and Chestnut streets.[12]

Nothing made so explicit the purpose of the Wainwright Building as the articles of association for the "Wainwright Real Estate Company," dated November 17, 1890. The company was incorporated "for pecuniary profit and gain" and capitalized at $700,000—a closely calculated figure, given that the costs of construction would come to $561,255, and together with the cost of the site would amount to a total of $688,255. Of the 7,000 shares issued at a par value of $100 per share, Catherine Wainwright held 4,450, representing an investment of $445,000, and Ellis Wainwright held 2,500, an investment of $250,000. William A. Haren, secretary of the Wainwright Brewery Company, held the remaining fifty shares. The three shareholders served as directors of the company.[13]

Adler & Sullivan reported the Wainwright Building commission at the end of November, and in a most routine manner, perhaps because they were associated with Ramsey late in the planning process. *The Economist,* a

Chicago real estate journal, mentioned first that the firm was planning the six-story Dooly Block in Salt Lake City, then continued:

> They are also making drawings for a nine-story office building, 114 × 127 feet, costing about $500,000, for a Mr. Wainwright to be erected in St. Louis, Mo. It will be fireproof and of steel construction. The material for the front has not yet been decided on.

Yet in fact the plan had been thoroughly worked out by November 7, and the *Globe-Democrat* had accurately reported even then that the fronts were to be of granite, sandstone, brick, and terra cotta.[14]

The various renderings of the Wainwright Building that were published in 1891 and 1892 emphasized its mass and stability, not an ecstasy of the vertical [22]. The first drawing appeared in an issue of *Inland Architect,* which had been published past schedule to serve as a memorial to John Root, who died at forty-one on January 15, 1891.[15]

Sullivan would boast later of a design "made in literally three minutes," as though from scratch, but Adler spoke more plainly about the immense task of making the working drawings for a tall building:

> The ordinary person has no idea of the care which must be exercised in drawing these plans. Separate

23. *Wainwright Tomb, St. Louis.*

drawings for the structural plans of every floor and every column must be made, showing the manner of riveting and joining together, how they must overlap, the bearings with which they must be provided, and a dozen other technicalities that might be named. . . . For the plans of the Wainwright building in St. Louis, which we designed and which is a plain business structure, was required the equal of one man's labor for eight months.[16]

Adler did not say how many draftsmen were involved, but the time needed for the drawings, together with what time may have elapsed before Ramsey associated with Adler & Sullivan, helped account for the unusual fact that the permit to construct a "10-story brick office building" was not issued until May 28, 1891—a year after Catherine Wainwright bought the site. Lost time amounted to an idle investment and lost revenue. Still another fact may have contributed to the delay: the death of Ellis Wainwright's wife on April 15, 1891. Charlotte Dickson Wainwright was ill for only a few days, and she was only thirty-four. Wainwright soon moved from their home at 3645 Delmar Avenue, and he never married again. In memory of his wife, he commissioned Adler & Sullivan to design a tomb for Bellefontaine Cemetery [23].[17]

A faint picture of the Wainwright Building under construction suffices to demolish Sullivan's claim to the "first authentic recognition and expression" of the metallic frame [24]. The photograph, ironically, was first published by Dankmar Adler. It shows a startling disparity between the tenuous metal frame, with its toothpicklike columns, and the immense mass of masonry in which the

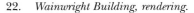

22. *Wainwright Building, rendering.*

frame seems imprisoned. If metal columns were to be hidden within masonry piers, John Root noted in 1890, the masonry properly served only to protect the metal against fire and the weather. He advocated a frame sheathed in terra cotta "supported at each story on the column itself by brackets." A few years later, Corydon T. Purdy reviewed the rapid progress of building technology; steel beams had been introduced in 1885, he observed, and more dependable metal members very soon led to a revolution in structure:

> In the old buildings, beams and columns were an adjunct to the masonry-work; in the new ones the relationship is reversed. The masonry walls are not needed for their strength.
>
> As the walls are supported at every floor [by the steel frame] the window areas may be made very much greater in the new buildings. . . . This increased window area is very important in smoky cities.[18]

The view of the Wainwright Building under construction exposes an unmitigated conflict between masonry and the metallic frame. It also shows that Sullivan's notion of Dionysian verticality contradicted the horizontal repetition of the office floors, the horizontal character of the structural bay, and the fact that each girder in section was nearly twice as large as the width of the columns. Not to mention that the entire enterprise bore no relation to an aspirant democracy. Sullivan's imposition of masonry enshrouded the structure and concealed in every way the essence of the tall office building.[19]

The upright members of the metallic frame were round columns of a very narrow section; they mocked the classical tradition of a noble masonry support akin to the human figure. Each column consisted of four riveted segments rolled by the Phoenix Iron Company of Phoenixville, Pennsylvania [25]. The company handbook published in 1890 asserted the virtues of the typical patented Phoenix column of wrought iron or steel:

> Wrought-iron or steel columns are coming into very general use in the construction of buildings, both on account of the saving of space that they afford when compared with heavy walls of masonry, and because of the great loads that are now to be provided for in large fire-proof buildings. In the latter case cast-iron columns are generally more costly and neither so safe nor so durable in case of fire.
>
> The Phoenix segmental column, circular in section, with ribbed flanges, provides the maximum of

24. *Wainwright Building in construction.*

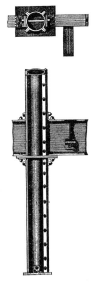

25. *Typical four-segment Phoenix column, plan and elevation.*

26. *Wainwright Building, fireproofed column in attic.*

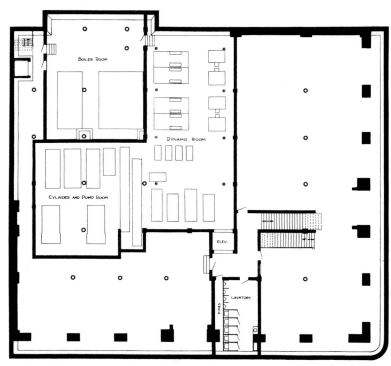

27. *Wainwright Building, basement plan.*

strength for load-bearing duty with a minimum of weight in the column itself. . . .

To carry a given load it requires the employment of the least amount of metal, and, on account of the simplicity of its construction, it is the cheapest as well as the best column offered to builders. . . .

Bearings for girders or beams at irregular heights are provided by projecting brackets that are properly secured to a segment, or by a plate passing transversely through the column between the flanges with seating angles along its upper edge.[20]

The handbook stated that steel columns (as those in the Wainwright Building were consistently said to be) possessed a load-bearing capacity 15 to 20 percent greater than comparable columns of wrought iron. The type used

in the Wainwright Building, designated "C," came in fourteen different standard sections, with an average outside diameter of only about 8½ inches [26]. The disparity between the thin, hollow Phoenix columns and the ponderous masonry piers could be seen as well in the basement plan [27]. Above ground, the massive corner piers of the building measured 7 feet 1½ inches wide on each face—ten times the width of the Phoenix columns within them.[21]

Such facts refute Sullivan's claim to having recognized and expressed metallic frame construction. Nor did he pay much attention to the plan. Instruction at the Ecole des Beaux Arts, he wrote, had amounted to "a theory of *plan*" and had failed to satisfy his quest for the "profound animus of a primal inspiration." As he continued to pursue emotional expression, the plan of the tall office building commanded nothing but his disdain:

These things . . . have to do strictly with the economics of the building, and I assume them to have been fully considered and disposed of to the satisfaction of purely utilitarian and pecuniary demands. Only in rare instances does the plan or floor arrangement of the tall office building take on an aesthetic value, and this usually when the lighting court is external or becomes an internal feature of great importance.

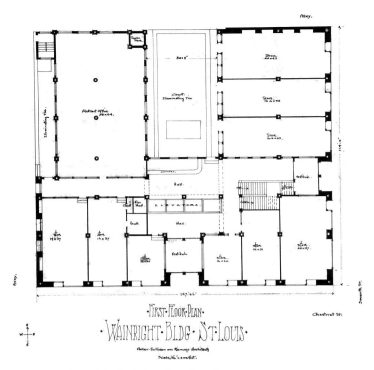

28. *Wainwright Building, first-floor plan.*

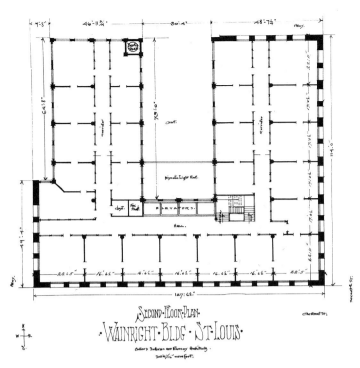

29. *Wainwright Building, second-floor plan.*

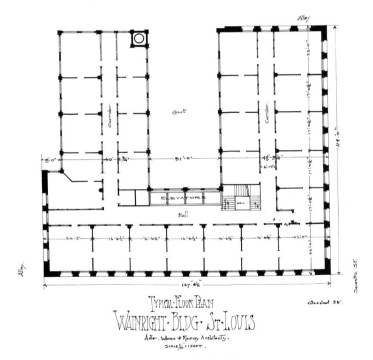

30. *Wainwright Building, plan of typical floor.*

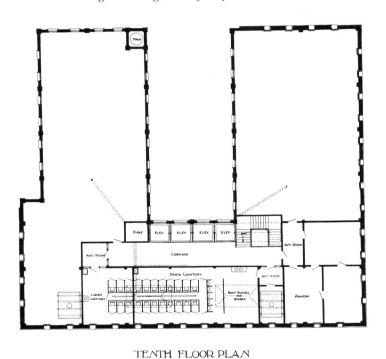

TENTH FLOOR PLAN

31. *Wainwright Building, attic plan.*

Yet it was precisely because the "purely utilitarian and pecuniary demands" constituted the fundamental conditions of the skyscraper that the floor plans of the Wainwright Building disclosed so much—not merely the size and arrangement of the offices, but how proportions had been determined by the way the building crowded its site and still gave space to light courts, how the classical regularity of the bays served to mask certain asymmetries, and how the densely clustered pilasters on both street-fronts so flagrantly discounted the great desideratum [28–31].[22]

The "economics of the building" pushed the plan to

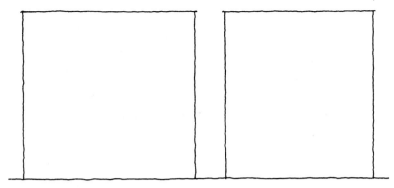

32. *Wainwright Building, outlines of south and east fronts.*

The plans also revealed that because the fronts reached to the lot-lines they entailed two anomalies. With seven bays, the principal front on Chestnut Street easily accommodated a centered entrance. But similar bays on Seventh Street could number only six, which put the east entrance off-center. More surprising, the bays of the secondary front measured 6 inches wider. Sullivan's small sketch for the terra cotta panels under the seventh-story sill disclosed the same fact; it specified two different widths, 6 feet ¼ inch for the panels of the east front and 5 feet 9¼ inches for those on the south [33]. The windows, correspondingly, were 3 inches wider on the east front. As

every lot-line to fully exploit the site. Thus the lateral dimensions of 127 feet 6½ inches on Chestnut Street and 114 feet on Seventh Street, as shown on the plans, had nothing to do with artistic proportions for the sake of emotional expression. In turn, the outlines of a building only 135 feet tall hardly suggested "a proud and soaring thing" [32].[23]

The purely utilitarian and pecuniary demands had also dictated the volume of the building in relation to the spaces left open. The small light court at the west wall (8 feet deep and 64 feet 8 inches long) and the principal light court at the north (31 by 73 feet) accounted for less than a fifth of the site; the building-mass occupied 11,760 square feet, or nearly 81 percent of the site.[24]

But a more important measure of efficiency was the ratio of net rentable space to a figure obtained by multiplying the area of the site by the number of rentable floors. On the first floor the plan showed a large abstract office and nine storefronts, with a total rental space of 7,817 square feet. The second through ninth floors numbered exactly 200 office spaces, or a total of 60,095 square feet. (Sullivan thought of the Wainwright Building as a nine-story structure, because the attic housed toilets and a barbershop but no office spaces.) In relation to the site-area multiplied by nine, the net rentable space or efficiency of the building thus came to 51.9 percent.[25]

The data of the plans demonstrated that the rentable space on the second through ninth floors multiplied that of the first floor by 7.69 times; the nature of the tall office building as a superimposition of floors, or what Sullivan dismissed as "stories of offices piled tier upon tier," could be precisely quantified. The offices connected to each other through doors in the partitions, and each office had at least two windows. Such was the pattern of horizontal interior space that Sullivan failed to express or even acknowledge in his "volcanic" conception of the streetfronts.[26]

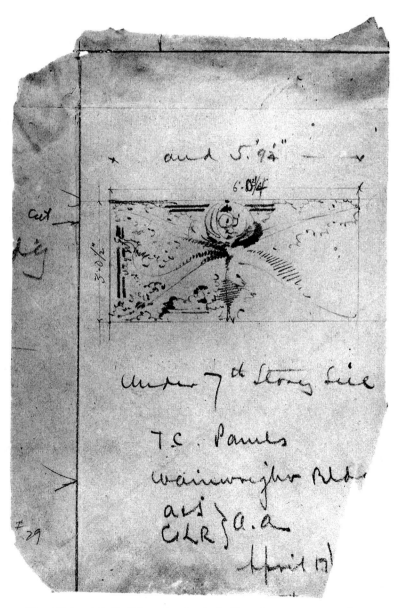

33. *Wainwright Building, drawing by Sullivan for terra cotta panels.*

34. *Wainwright Building, east front.*

if he knew somehow that over the years the lesser front usually would be the more visible, Sullivan stated the width of the east panels first [34].[27]

The floor plans showed the masonry pattern of the façades turning the corners to extend to the light courts.

Finally, they expressed something of the massiveness of the corner piers. In choosing to emphasize the sense of stability by exaggerating the masonry of the corners, Sullivan unfortunately diminished the largest and most desirable offices; he rendered the corners opaque and

35. *Wainwright Building, corner office.*

lifeless [35]. The superiority of even a bare mercantile structure such as the Willoughby Building was apparent [36]. In his obstruction of light at the corners, Sullivan turned a blind eye not only to the sacrifice of floor space to light courts but to all the light-gathering efforts of the glass doors, transoms, and windows of the vestibules and corridors [37–39].[28]

He also flouted his own pronouncement that the "true work of the architect is to organize, integrate and glorify UTILITY." In taking the street elevations as his opportunity to express democracy and nature, Sullivan glossed over the basic economic function of decorated streetfronts, that of attracting tenants. By contrast, the maiden issue of *Architectural Record* acknowledged the connection between commerce and the increased enrichment of buildings with artistic terra cotta:

36. *Willoughby Building, corner office.*

37.   *Wainwright Building, vestibule.*

38.   *Wainwright Building, seventh-floor corridor.*

39.   *Wainwright Building, seventh-floor doors and paneling.*

The evidences of the material prosperity of this country are probably more fully displayed in its street architecture than in any other manner. With the marvelous increase in real estate values during the past twenty years there has been a coincident growth in the size and decoration of its buildings.

Daniel Burnham, in whom Sullivan generously found the dream-imagination, put the matter more directly. "Beauty has always paid better than any other commodity," he said in 1897, "and always will."[29]

At street level, strangely enough, the Wainwright Building for the most part possessed an austere rigor [40]. Its base conveyed a sense of immovable solidity, yet paradoxically emphasized the horizontal as if to accompany traffic along the sidewalks and streets. Both qualities contradicted the vaunted thrust of the Dionysian vertical. Nor did the carefully worked masonry of granite and sandstone and terra cotta give any hint of the underlying metallic frame or the revolution in the structure of tall buildings. Instead, the wall drew close to what Wright would critique as the "old order" of a lingering, fortress-like classicism:

> Outside and inside were usually quite separate, wholly independent of each other. Holes were cut into the block-mass at intervals for a little light and some

air: the deeper the hole looked to be, that is to say the thicker the sides of the hole were—the architects called these sides the "reveal"—the better.[30]

The exterior effects of the base depended on a compounding of the first two stories that assigned to the second floor a most ambiguous role. If, in his skyscraper formula, only the first story could be said "to differ in function from its successors," the critic Montgomery Schuyler once told Sullivan, then the grouping of two stories into a base may well have derived from an instinctive desire to maintain "inherited notions of proportion." The projecting sillcourse and strong shadow-line clearly separated the second story of the Wainwright Building from the stories above.

Early tall buildings in Chicago had commonly boasted a second story of prime rental space, and in his 1896 essay Sullivan indeed wrote that the second story should be "readily accessible by stairways." John Root had said in 1890 that even a three-story base could represent a rational response to "the question of revenue" because the second floor gained value by being accessible from stairs, and the third floor was "apt, like the second, to be occupied by large corporations, or other tenants requiring considerable space in one room." But in the Wainwright Building the second-floor plan was just like that of the other floors; and the rental brochure, in stating that a

40. *Wainwright Building, base.*

41.   *Wainwright Building, east entrance.*

42.   *Wainwright Building, carved sandstone at south entrance.*

43.   *Wainwright Building, carved sandstone at east entrance.*

basement lavatory would serve the first floor, implied that the second floor would join all those above it in being served by the "separate lavatories for ladies and for gentlemen on the tenth floor."[31]

Sullivan took great interest in treating the entrances as bowers of densely entwined ornamentation [41–43]. The patterns were carved into sandstone but were more suggestive of modeling in clay—which, according to Wright, was always Sullivan's basic medium of expression. In the outer faces they evoked both the fertility of plant life and a more geometric or nuclear order of natural energy. But the swirling frenzy on the inner faces seemed more symbolic of the uncontrolled and predacious tendencies of nature. Inside, the doorknobs and doorplates were adorned with a more conventional interlacement of the

44. *Wainwright Building, doorplate and doorknob.*

45. *Wainwright Building, façade detail.*

letters "W" and "B," as well as numerals to record the year construction began [44].[32]

An upward glance at either façade—especially if recorded by a camera unable to correct the vertical lines into parallels—might lend credence to Sullivan's notion of a proud and soaring thing. But a straightforward and more considered view shows that he had created instead a colossal, oppressive portcullis of masonry over what he unhappily called the "office-cells" [45]. When he treated the mullions as seven-story pilasters identical to the piers, he ignored the tenuity of the metallic frame, obscured the bay structure, and concealed the size and shape of each office. Ironically, the doubling of the pilasters, intended to reinforce and quicken the rhythm of the Dionysian vertical, only broadened the amount of masonry in the walls and made them all the more ponderous. A street perspective could altogether hide the windows [46].[33]

By 1891, when construction of the Wainwright Building got under way, Corydon T. Purdy could already speak of masonry walls as an expression from the past:

> At first so much glass in the front of a great building and so little solid surface was a novelty, and its appearance of weakness in contrast with the older, heavier buildings drew forth a quite general disapproval. This distrust is unfounded, and those who build and will inform themselves on the real merits of the question are ready to demand the light, and object to the loss of income due to great areas of masonry.

Phoenix columns, so thin and strong, could serve perfectly the demand for more light, and they suggested an enclosing structure completely different from that of the Wainwright Building. In his disregard for the great desideratum, Sullivan also betrayed his inattention to the elementary conceptual opposition of a mural building to a skeletal structure of narrow piers. His failure to discriminate between constructive principles appeared as well in *Kindergarten Chats*:

> . . . you may look on the wall as a lengthened pier or on the pier as a shortened wall; it does not signify. The essence of each is that it is a vertical mass resting on the ground, and capable of support.[34]

The pilasters of the Wainwright Building, 2 feet 6 inches wide, exceeded the width of the Phoenix columns by more than three times. Contrary to what Sullivan claimed, his streetfronts obscured the anatomy and pur-

46. *Wainwright Building, view from Chestnut Street, looking east.*

. . . it already aspires, for it rises vertically from its ground-support into the air. . . . While it seems aspiring, it seems also solidly founded: it impresses us as immovable, as static: as timeless. . . . We might, for pictorial purposes, have presupposed our pier as a tree trunk.

But if the pier aspired and brought to mind the growth of a tree, how could it be at the same time static, timeless, immovable? Such were the perils and confusions in Sullivan's program of metaphorical representation.[35]

By ornamenting the terra cotta spandrels with motifs from nature, Sullivan did little to lighten the masonry walls; and by advancing all the pilasters, whether mullions or piers, he broke the spandrels into a staccato pattern without relation to the depth of the girders, the width of the bays, or the disposition of office spaces. He essentially divorced the garment of the building from the structure, the interior, and its function. And his inventiveness in surface decoration, what he described as "intricate and involved foliation and efflorescence," could not reasonably become the primary inspiriting force in the architecture of a tall office building.[36]

When he composed the middle stories of the Wainwright Building with redoubled pilasters and ornamental spandrel panels, Sullivan gave the typical office bay an enclosure more than two-thirds opaque [47]. In his effort to "vitalize" building materials, as he put it, and "infuse into them the true life of the people," he remained bound to the values of the traditional masonry wall. Thus his response to the problem of the tall office building was not a radical or even a rational solution. On the east front, where the typical bay measured slightly more than 17 feet wide, each window pane was only 51½

47. *Wainwright Building, diagram of typical bay, south front.*

pose of the building. For even an unadorned pier appealed to him mainly as an agent of symbolic expression:

inches wide; on the south front the panes were only 48½ inches wide. Even if one conceded a preference for masonry and an affection for Sullivan's idiom of naturalistic decoration, any reasonable design of the office bay would have narrowed both the mullions and the piers in order to embrace three or more windows [48].[37]

48. *Wainwright Building, diagram of conjectural bay.*

49. *Wainwright Building, attic detail.*

By confessing his delight in the "completing power and luxuriance of the attic," Sullivan spoke volumes [49, 50]. Because the attic merely housed toilets, mechanical equipment, storage space, and a skylighted barbershop, it escaped the claims of the great desideratum. That left it free to serve Sullivan's desire for a gigantic capital on top of the shaft and base of the building:

> This brings us to the attic, which, having no division into office-cells, and no special requirement for lighting, gives us the power to show by means of its broad expanse of wall, and its dominating weight and character, that which is the fact,—namely, that the series of office tiers has come definitely to an end.

Hence he masked the most utilitarian and humble functions of the building with his greatest "luxuriance" of ornamentation, a final flourish of tangled plant forms that imposed its "dominating weight and character" on top of the insistent and opposite pattern of the pilasters. And what was the frieze meant to say? That democracy and nature could reach no higher?[38]

50. *Wainwright Building, attic window, east front.*

SULLIVAN AND AUTHENTICITY

Louis Sullivan's self-appraisal as the first architect to master the problem of the tall office building finds little support in the Wainwright Building. What he said about the building does not conform to fact, and the metaphorical program he put forth in his writing neither inhered in the skyscraper as a new building type nor was achieved by his architecture.[1]

Sullivan said that in his years with Adler he was the partner in charge of "the aesthetics." He also said the aesthetic solution to an architectural problem would come from a "spontaneous, powerful and unerring" emotional response. And so far as he was concerned, the "function" of the skyscraper became exactly what the dream-imagination asked from civilization, an expression of man's "aspirant emotions."[2]

Yet the Wainwright Building stood very heavily upon the ground [51]. Even so light a touch as John Edelmann's could mislead the editors of *Engineering Magazine* into attributing the design to H. H. Richardson [52]. Not without reason, of course, because the Field Wholesale Store had greatly reinforced Sullivan's devotion to the ponderous masonry wall. Sullivan called Richardson's building an oration, "the outpouring of a copious, direct, large and simple mind":

> Buildings such as this, and there are not many of them, stand as landmarks, as promontories, to the navigator. They show when and where architecture has taken on its outburst of form as a grand passion. . . . It refreshes and strengthens, because it is elemental, bespeaks the largeness and the bounty of nature, the manliness of man.[3]

The price Sullivan paid to prolong the masonry wall was far too great. His fronts for the Wainwright Building may have appeared decisive, coherent, even classically correct, but they dissembled structure, space, function, the thirst for light, and the very nature of the skyscraper. Sullivan said the tall office building stood as "something new under the sun." But to the new architectural type he simply applied a traditional architectural formula.[4]

When he told Bragdon the "structures prior to the Wainwright were in my 'masonry' period," he implied that the "volcanic design" left behind all his earlier work. Yet the truth was nearly opposite. So far as responding to the great desideratum and to the purposes of the metallic frame construction, Sullivan regressed. Two of his buildings that stood side by side in Chicago told the story more faithfully [53]. The modest Borden Block of 1880–81, unlike the Schiller Theater Building of 1891–92, did not aspire to a monumental masonry expression, did not affect to be a proud and soaring thing, and did not adopt an overscaled entablature surmounted by a trivial cupola. Instead, it answered the call for light.[5]

In 1892, John Edelmann said rather more than he intended when he mocked American commercial buildings in which "the supposed necessity for light and the use of cast-iron have resulted in a class of structures 'without visible means of support.'" For in fact the skeletal frame performed marvelously in serving space and light and the economics of commercial architecture. Sullivan surely knew its advantages; why else would he boast of having given steel-frame construction its "first authentic recognition and expression in the exterior treatment of the Wainwright Building, a nine-story office structure"? Moreover, he wrote that the heroes of his early years were railroad-bridge engineers: men who faced problems squarely. But he came to think the engineering mind was too literal. Sullivan recalled that as he matured his values changed:

> In childhood his idols had been the big strong men who *did* things. Later on he had begun to feel the greater power of men who could *think* things; later the expansive power of men who could *imagine* things; and at last he began to recognize as dominant, the will of the Creative Dreamer: he who possessed the power of vision needed to harness Imagination, to harness the intellect, to make science do his will, to make the emotions serve him— for without emotion nothing.[6]

Without emotion nothing: Sullivan's doctrine of emotional expression turned upside down the dictum *Ars sine*

51. *Wainwright Building, looking northwest.*

Frank Lloyd Wright, Louis Sullivan and the Skyscraper

THE WAINWRIGHT BUILDING, ST. LOUIS—RICHARDSON, ARCHITECT.

52. *Wainwright Building, rendering.*

53. *Schiller Building (left) and Borden Block, Chicago. Both demolished.*

scientia nihil est (Art without knowledge is nothing), uttered at a building conference for the Cathedral of Milan in 1400. From his student days abroad he instead remembered Rome. He said his encounter with Michelangelo's frescoes of the Sistine Chapel led him to conclude that "Imagination passes beyond reason and is a consummated act of Instinct—the primal power of Life at work." If instinct and emotion were to overwhelm intellect, that would be because the continuously operative law of nature impels every entity to seek and find its form "by virtue of its working plan, or purpose or utility; or, if you choose to say so, by virtue of its desire to live and to express itself." Again, function had become self-expression, and Sullivan could see in buildings "the objective possibilities of subjective impulses." When a building was made to serve as the image of man's "desire to procreate his own personality," its function was changed into an architect's opportunity for emotional expression. Sullivan intended to project his volatile self into the streetfronts of a building to somehow make it speak for aspirant democracy, because the dream-imagination found its purpose "in the upbuilding into visible fact of the great World-Dream, Democracy."[7]

Such a program also entailed the belief that the vast materialism of American life, as Sullivan wrote, signified both a "gestation period of spirituality" and the "coming release of the heart from its bondage to the intellect." Now he chose to style himself not an architect, not even a "*poet who uses not words but building materials as a medium of expression,*" but a seer and prophet of "the gospel of democracy, the motive power of the world."[8]

Sullivan could say he valued spiritual results only, but the palpable everyday truth of the tall office building bore no relation to his sententious pronouncements on emotional expression, the primacy of the subjective or the world-dream of democracy. So far as expression, the "dominant chord" of the Wainwright Building was its brooding reddish color harmony, not loftiness. The idea of the skyscraper as a soaring thing existed already in the hyperbole of the word itself; and "skyscraper" at least stood happily free of pretensions to the spiritual. Skyscrapers, simply put, were tall and conspicuous—as John J. Flinn noted in celebrating the city of Chicago in advance of the World's Columbian Exposition of 1893:

> To-day the office buildings of Chicago rise up in every direction. They do more than rise up. They tower, and some of them seem to soar.[9]

54. *Monadnock Block, Chicago, rendering.*

55. *Monadnock Block, east front.*

When he wrote of "slenderness and aspiration, the soaring quality as of a thing rising from the earth as a unitary utterance," Sullivan more accurately described the Monadnock Block than any building of his own. The *Inland Architect* published a rendering of the Monadnock Block in November 1889, many months—perhaps even more than a year—before Sullivan conceived the fronts for the Wainwright Building, and the sixteen-story office building from Burnham & Root was constructed at the southwest corner of Dearborn and Jackson streets, only four blocks from the Auditorium [54, 55]. Sullivan mistakenly remembered it as a structure of "solid masonry," and in writing of its "amazing cliff of brickwork, rising sheer and stark, with a subtlety of line and surface, a direct singleness of purpose, that gave one the thrill of romance," he failed to remark how aggressively the windows asserted their place and caught the light on three fronts. Nor did he acknowledge that by informing the Monadnock Block with a vitality like that of a tall plant, John Root gave a more inward and true meaning to the ideal of organic expression.[10]

Root warned that the circumstances of the new building type called for forms adapted to the expression "of new ideas and new aspects of life":

> . . . the arbitrary dicta of self-constituted architectural prophets should have no voice. Every one of these problems should be rationally worked out alone, and each should express the character and the aims of the people about it.

Dankmar Adler discerned that the traditional refractory materials of construction could no longer dictate the creation of form, and that the new materials would tend to free architectural design:

> The architect is not allowed to wait until, seized by an irresistible impulse from within, he gives the world the fruit of his studies and musings. He is of the world as well as in it . . . and he is pressed into its service and must work for it and with it, no matter whether or not urged by the spirit within him. . . .
>
> I wish to maintain that the steel pillar and beam and other contemporary contributions to the materials and processes of building construction, that the modern business building, and many other so-called monstrosities, are as legitimate contributions to architectural art, as were in their day, when first introduced, the stone pier and lintel, the brick wall or pier, the arch, the vault. . . .
>
> Let us then welcome the prosaic output of furnace and mill, and even the unpromising and garish sheet of plate glass. If they are always used where they are wanted and as they are wanted . . . we shall have taken the first step toward the transmutation of these utterances of scientific prose into the language of poetry and art.[11]

At the time that Adler saluted the new materials of construction, in 1896, he knew the first step already had been taken by the Tacoma Building, and the second by the Reliance Building—a more handsome structure, and surely the skyscraper that best expressed its time and all the conditions of its existence [56]. The Reliance Building stood 65 feet taller than the Wainwright Building and still its corner pier measured only 2½ feet wide (twice the width of the metal column, not ten times), while its mullions were hardly a fourth as wide as

56. *Reliance Building, Chicago, east front.*

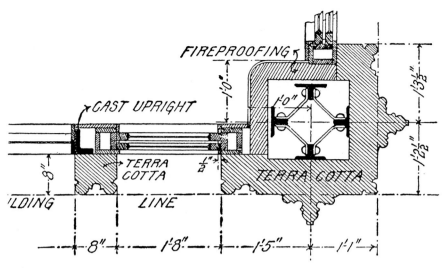

57.   *Reliance Building, plan of corner pier and mullion.*

those of Sullivan's building [57]. Details such as those proved how fresh the architecture of the tall building could be when rationally conceived, free from the weight of tradition.[12]

The Reliance Building above all heralded a new architecture of glass. With its metallic frame fireproofed in white-enameled terra cotta, the "balance of the front," as the *Economist* said in 1894, was destined to be "all plate glass." The building also expressed its true nature as a tall stack of horizontal floors of space for rent. Only 56 feet wide at the State Street front and 85 feet deep on Washington Street, it towered above the sidewalks without any forcing of a Dionysian vertical. Its ornamental

scheme, finally, attempted to signify nothing but a kinship with the great skeletal structures of the Gothic era.[13]

A tall office building well considered, Henry Van Brunt wrote in 1889, would be "flooded with light in every part." The thirst for light rendered wholly irrelevant Sullivan's affection for the monumental effects of a masonry wall. So, too, did the obvious disparity between the huge size of a skyscraper and its minimal claim to civic or commemorative meaning. How ironic that Sullivan would boast of his abilities "to sense and to discern what lay behind the veil of appearances" and yet attempt to veil the skyscraper—that "stark, staring exclamation of eternal strife"—in a specious cloak of spirituality.[14]

WRIGHT AND LIGHT

In 1893, when he set out on his own, Frank Lloyd Wright first remodeled his offices in the Schiller Building for the sake of light. He changed each door into "a single clear plate of glass," he recalled much later, and installed a patterned ceiling screen to diffuse artificial light as if it were sunlight. Wright kept alert to light in all the years to come, and he continued to associate light with the tall office building. As he looked through old drawings in 1951, he playfully noted that a light-grille for his Oak Park studio of 1898 and a lamp standard for the Henry J. Allen house of 1915–18 could easily be transformed into designs for skyscrapers.[1]

Wright's first skyscraper project, an 1897 streetfront composed of translucent Luxfer Prisms, was based entirely on light [58]. Because the project was intended to advertise the glass prisms, he let the part become the motif for the whole; squares within squares, all reflecting the shape of the prisms, established the grid of the bays. Certain details were suffused with a strong sense of Sullivan's ornament, but the whole point of the Luxfer project was to cast daylight into the farthest reaches of every office.[2]

The fronts of the Wainwright Building had nevertheless impressed Wright deeply. After all, the years during which he served as a "good pencil" in Sullivan's hand and revered him as the "ideal iconoclast" counted those during which the Wainwright Building was conceived and constructed. In two of the most important of his own early buildings, Wright lightly echoed Sullivan's façade rhythm of pilasters framed by broadened corner piers. In both projects, however, he wanted to isolate the interior space from an unpleasant street environment by depending on a central skylight rather than peripheral windows for illumination. Thus he described the Larkin Administration Building of 1903–06 in Buffalo, New York, as "a single large room in which the main floors are galleries open to a large central court . . . lighted from above" [59–61]. Wright never intended to make an office building a mere signboard for occult metaphorical representations:

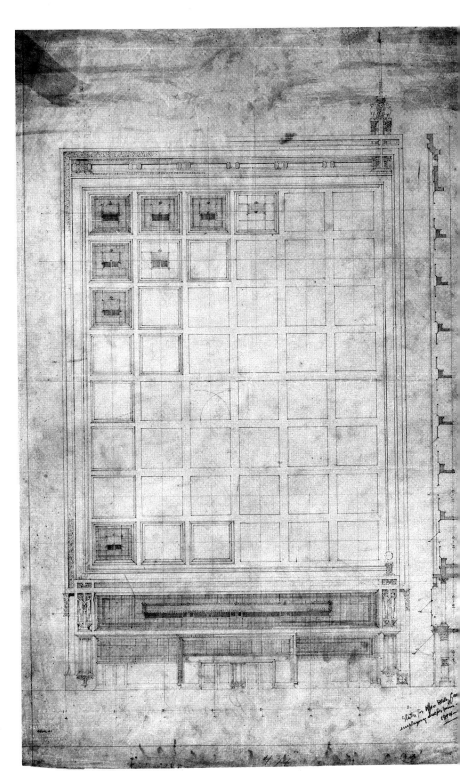

58. *Luxfer Prism project, façade.*

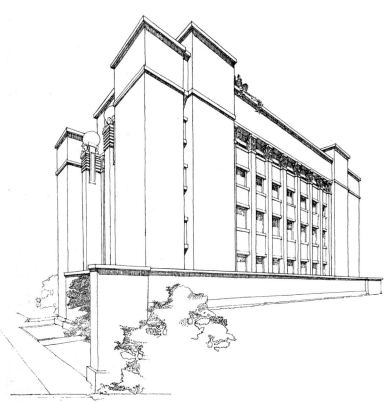

59. *Larkin Building, Buffalo, New York. Demolished.*

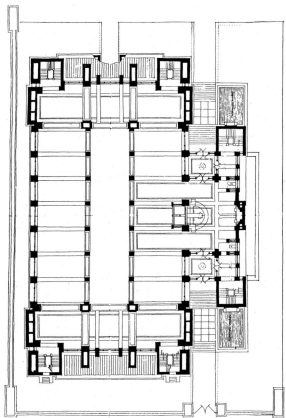

60. *Larkin Building, plan above window sills.*

It was built to house the commercial engine of the Larkin Company in light, wholesome, well-ventilated quarters. . . . The building is a simple working out of certain utilitarian conditions, its exterior a simple cliff of brick. . . . All the windows of the various stories or "galleries" are seven feet above the floor, the space beneath being used for steel filing cabinets. . . . The entrance vestibules, from either street and from the main lobby, together with the toilet accommodations and the rest rooms for employees, are all located in an annex, which intercepts the light from the main office as little as possible. . . . Here, again, most of the critic's "architecture" has been left out. Therefore the work may have the same claim to consideration as a "work of art" as an ocean liner, a locomotive or a battle ship.

This left any hint of the spiritual to the light of the central court and to the moralisms—some from the Bible, others provided more immediately from the office manager, William R. Heath—displayed on the walls. Wright found his greatest satisfaction when he articulated the

building-mass by giving a definite independence to the corner stairtowers. This too he achieved through a detail of lighting, the narrow vertical rifts filled with glass. When he designed the Unity Temple of 1905–08 in Oak Park, Illinois, he again took light to be the principal theme; and again he used light in narrow slots, or rifts, to liberate the corners [62, 63].[3]

In his first complete design for a skyscraper, projected for the *San Francisco Call*, Wright so exaggerated the cantilevered cornice, the rhythm of the pilasters, and the Dionysian rush to verticality that he virtually parodied the Wainwright Building [64, 65]. The driving idea, unlike Sullivan's, was nevertheless structural; the drawings presented an essay in reinforced concrete and earthquake-resistant construction. All the circumstances pointed Wright in that direction.

On one drawing Wright later noted that he had collaborated with Harrison Albright, a Los Angeles architect. Albright had already benefited from a large number of commissions from John D. Spreckels, the owner of the *Call* and a son of Claus Spreckels, the "Sugar King." Although the younger Spreckels maintained a house in

61. *Larkin Building, light court.*

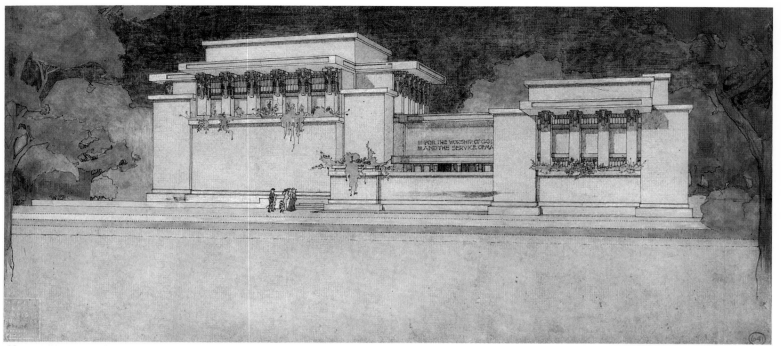

62. *Unity Temple, Oak Park, Illinois.*

63. *Unity Temple, interior, looking south.*

64. *San Francisco* Call *project, perspective study.*

65. *San Francisco* Call *project, rendering.*

San Francisco, he spent most of his time in San Diego, where he owned office buildings, the street railways, the water supply, and the newspapers, as well as Coronado Island and its celebrated resort hotel. To keep track of his work for Spreckels, Albright traveled once a week to an office in San Diego.[4]

It was there by chance that he met and hired Wright's son John, then nineteen years old. A kindly man, Albright sympathized with John's embarrassment over the publicity that attended his father's extramarital love-life at Taliesin, the home and studio Wright had just built near Spring Green, Wisconsin. Albright let John take charge of a fresh commission from Spreckels, a three-story workingman's hotel. More than forty years later, John was proud to recall that his drawings for the hotel were distinctly modernist:

> All structures by Mr. Albright were re-inforced concrete and all buildings, except for the Golden West Hotel, were of traditional design in Mr. Albright's characteristic arrangement of imitation quoins, cartouches, Greek balustrades, columns and egg and dart molded cornices all neatly trimmed like his meticulous Van Dyke.

John decided his calling was architecture. On July 4, 1912, he wrote his father:

> Now that I have charge of Harrison Albright's San Diego office—I will ask you, probably for the last time, for a position with you.
> 1st. Because you are my Father.
> 2nd. I admire your Architecture.
> 3rd. I am and will be able to help you.

But it must have been a second letter, dated July 19, that caught Wright's eye:

> Mr. Albright has over a million dollars worth of work under construction in San Diego at the present time and his Theatre Bldg. (6 stories high, covering nearly a square block) will be finished by the middle of next month. His work is all reinforced concrete and he takes nothing under $100,000.
> I am sending a few pictures of our little house (Mr. Gill's work).

The little house was one John shared with his older brother Lloyd, who had begun working for the architect Irving J. Gill earlier that year. Twenty years before, Gill had worked with Frank Lloyd Wright in the offices of Adler & Sullivan. Gill, too, was designing buildings in San Diego of reinforced concrete.[5]

Reinforced concrete could easily be masked by a veneer of traditional architectural motifs and materials. In a manifesto delivered at Hull-House in 1901, Wright had defined the modern tall office building as the "machine pure and simple," and had asserted that "the deadly struggle taking place here [in Chicago] between the machine and the art of structural tradition reveals 'art' torn and hung upon the steel frame of commerce, a forlorn head upon a pike." Only a few years later, *Architectural Record* presented the Ingalls Building of

Cincinnati as the first skyscraper in reinforced concrete— "a concrete box of 8-inch walls, with concrete floors and roof, concrete beams, concrete columns, concrete stairs . . . a complete concrete monolith." The monolith nonetheless resided behind a cloak of marble, glazed brick, and glazed terra cotta. Wright shortly designed a concrete factory in Chicago; he faced the structure with brick, but left the walls plain as could be. He soon built Unity Temple not in brick, as originally intended, but in exposed concrete.[6]

Apart from the promise of concrete as a material potentially expressive of modernism stood its claim to strength in resisting earthquakes. Wright learned in 1911 of a chance to build a major hotel in Tokyo, a place notoriously vulnerable to earthquakes. Then came the skyscraper design for the *San Francisco Call* in a city more than half destroyed by the great earthquake of April 18, 1906, and three days of ensuing fires: a disaster, wrote Henry Ericsson much later, that "put architects and builders to school with a seriousness and a sense of responsibility never before or since equaled." Louis Sullivan spent three weeks in San Francisco ostensibly to study the damage; he was also badly in need of work. On his return to Chicago he stopped in Kansas City, where he praised the strength of the metallic frame:

> The calamity does not call for any new methods of building construction. The modern steel, coherent, well-anchored structure is the best, and will stand any earthquake shock except one of such a nature as would depopulate the city. It has already been tested by fire, but never under such conditions as at San Francisco, where no water was used. That it withstood this most severe test is conclusive evidence that it cannot be improved upon.[7]

Prominent among the metallic frame structures that famously survived the earthquake stood the Claus Spreckels Building of 1895–98, designed in part as a home for the *Call* and thus commonly known as the Call Building [66]. A domed and ornate pile, it towered above its neighbors along Market Street, the grand diagonal reaching southwest toward Twin Peaks, as the tallest building in the city. An official survey after the disaster found it "one of the best-designed skeleton buildings in San Francisco," harmed primarily by fire, which destroyed wood floors and damaged marble tiles and wainscoting. A few years later, *Building and Industrial News* said there was only one reinforced concrete building in the city at the time of the great earthquake, and it was still under construction, but that other concrete structures within the broad path of destruction performed so well that 128 reinforced concrete buildings could be counted in San Francisco only four years later. Ernest L. Ransome, the pioneer of concrete construction in California, boasted in 1912 that his own work at Stanford University had withstood the great earthquake "with little if any damage." Reinforced concrete became the building material of the hour.[8]

Wright's perspective studies show his concrete skyscraper for the *Call* sited close to the Claus Spreckels Building and slightly farther up Market Street. The stretch of Market Street from Third Street to Fourth Street, surprisingly, measures more than 825 feet; Wright's skyscraper would have appeared east of the juncture with O'Farrell Street. One of his schemes entails a wing connecting to the Claus Spreckels Building, but in any case the new tower would have stepped back and away from the older skyscraper with very little deference. It would have become the tallest skyscraper in the city, and its astonishingly cantilevered cornices and balconies would have overwhelmed the massive fourteen-story cornice of the Claus Spreckels Building, which by means of complicated brackets projected more than five feet beyond the walls [67].

Wright described the *Call* project only briefly and many years later: "To be run in concrete same as a grain elevator is constructed. Projecting slab at top is lighting fixture to illuminate the walls. Building set back so overhang covers only own ground-space."[9]

66. *Claus Spreckels Building, San Francisco.*

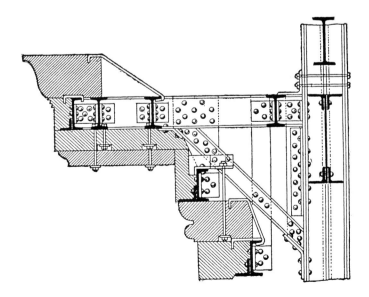

67. *Claus Spreckels Building, cantilever bracket.*

Night lights from the dramatic cantilever slabs could have advertised the *Call*, but the plans give no evidence that Wright ever discussed with Spreckels or even with Albright the requirements of a newspaper [68]. Instead, the plans show the tall first story partitioned into a series of narrow shops, with no sign of reception areas or counting rooms. They designate the top three stories as club rooms, much as in Burnham & Root's Masonic Temple of 1890–92. The typical floor plan for offices lacks any hint of newspaper functions or spaces. Given a front on Market Street measuring less than a fourth the length of

the side elevations, the interior spaces take on a shape far from satisfactory for large offices or a metropolitan newsroom. Yet the elongated plan meant that Wright could eliminate interior columns by adopting a structural system of closely spaced piers at the perimeter, with massive cross-walls for wind bracing and further resistance to earthquakes. Essentially, the building would have been a tube structure.[10]

Certain details prefigured Wright's drawings for the Imperial Hotel in Tokyo and what he described as its "perforated roof slabs becoming decorative cornices, other

68. *San Francisco project, plans for main floor (bottom), typical floors, and top floors.*

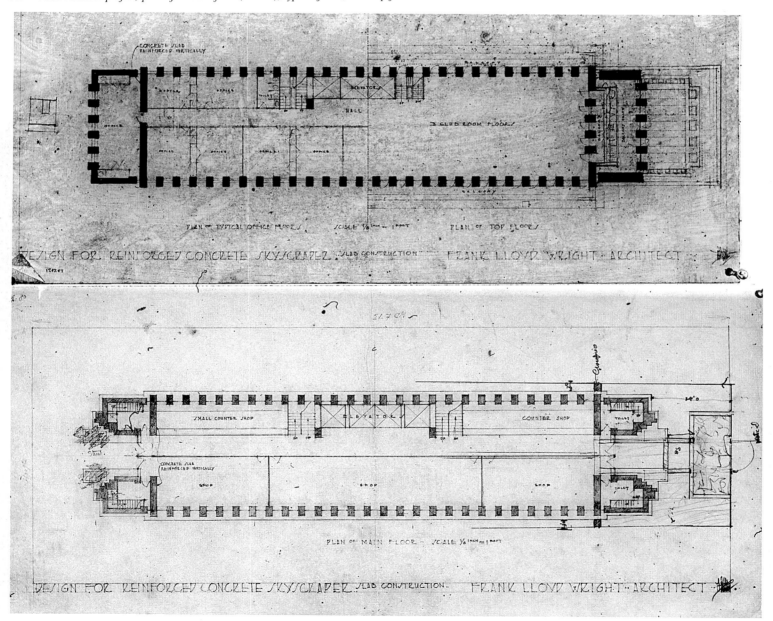

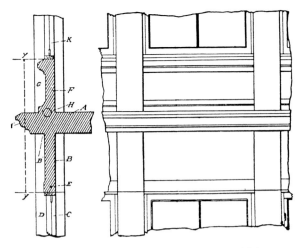

69. *Patented system for spandrels and cantilevered beltcourse.*

floor slabs becoming balconies, canopies, flying bridges, etc." But in the *Call* project Wright failed to explore the full capabilities of reinforced concrete construction; he had not yet seized the idea implicit in the system Ransome patented in 1902 for building factories [69]. It extended the floor slab past the perimeter columns and into a cantilevered beltcourse. The resulting curtain walls, Ransome wrote in 1912, meant that "large window areas are easily made possible."[11]

What little can be learned about the *Call* project suggests that John Wright introduced his father to Albright, whether directly or through correspondence. Subsequently, when Albright heard from Spreckels that a new building for the *Call* might be undertaken, he unofficially asked Wright to design a reinforced concrete skyscraper of about twenty-five stories. All too soon, however, Wright's drawings either were rejected by the client (who had never directly commissioned them) or were nullified by the fact that Spreckels chose the Reid Bros. of San Francisco as his architects. Certainly the Reid Bros. had a great advantage; they had designed the Claus Spreckels Building as well as a newspaper building for the *Oregonian* in Portland, mansions in San Francisco for both Spreckels and his father, and even the Hotel del Coronado in San Diego. When they reported their work at the beginning of 1913, the Reid Bros. made no mention of a tower for the *Call*, but on March 21 the newspaper announced its plans for a twenty-five-story skyscraper at the southeast corner of Fourth and Market streets—the busiest place in America, it said, after Forty-second Street and Broadway in New York and State and Madison streets in Chicago. The plans were from the Reid Bros., and the finished rendering that appeared in the newspaper was published widely.[12]

But the Reid Bros. fared hardly any better than Wright and Albright in seeing their plans realized. M. H. de Young, who with his brother had founded the *Chronicle* in 1865, bought the *Call* to eliminate a competing morning newspaper. He closed it on August 31, 1913. When the *Call* miraculously reappeared the next day, it was an afternoon daily published by F. W. Kellogg of Pasadena, who had engineered the entire maneuver. Spreckels retained only a twenty-percent interest in the paper and relinquished an active role in its publication. A reinforced-concrete building designed by the Reid Bros. was constructed for the *Call* at the southwest corner of New Montgomery and Jessie streets, behind the Palace Hotel. It stood only seven stories tall.[13]

In the spring of 1914, when Wright showed a handsome model of his concrete skyscraper at the twenty-seventh annual exhibition of the Chicago Architectural Club, he titled it simply "Office Building, San Francisco" [70]. The

70. *Model for San Francisco skyscraper project.*

project for the *Call* had "never progressed beyond the sketch and model stage," John Wright recalled in 1953. That was enough, however, to show how far Wright had been misled by the Wainwright Building and Sullivan's bluff of having solved the artistic problem of the modern tall office building. (The motif of the principal entrance, moreover, presented a rectilinear reduction of Sullivan's compound arches in the "Golden Door" of the Transportation Building at the World's Columbian Exposition of 1893 in Chicago.) But if the clustered piers of Wright's project for a concrete skyscraper opposed the need for abundant light, at least they represented a structural response not only to earthquakes but to the problem of the tall building.[14]

Wright regarded architecture as an art founded on fertile principles, not formulas, and propelled by moments of wondrous invention. Yet even as he reached beyond Sullivan's formula for the tall office building he proved slow to arrive at a more penetrating appraisal of the Wainwright Building. Wright had grasped a radically different idea of the skyscraper by the time of Sullivan's death in 1924, but still he wrote of the Wainwright Building as though everything Sullivan said about it had been true:

> When he brought in the board with the motive of the Wainwright Building outlined in profile and in scheme upon it and threw it down on my table, I was perfectly aware of what had happened. This was Louis Sullivan's greatest moment—his greatest effort. The "skyscraper," as a new thing beneath the sun, an entity with virtue, individuality and beauty all its own, was born.
>
> Until Louis Sullivan showed the way the masses of the tall buildings were never a complete whole in themselves. They were ugly, harsh aggregates with no sense of unity, fighting tallness instead of accepting it. What unity those masses now have, that pile upward toward New York and Chicago skies, is due to the Master-mind that first perceived one as a harmonious unit—its height triumphant.
>
> The Wainwright Building cleared the way and to

this day remains the master key to the skyscraper as a matter of architecture in the work of the world.[15]

Wright told the same story many times. When he lectured at Princeton University in 1930, however, he denounced "landlord *profits* in a dull craze for verticality and vertigo" and the "shrieking verticality" that sold "perpendicularity to the earthworms in the village lane below." Verticality, he said, was "already stale." As to the Wainwright Building, he faulted its roof-slab for serving as an emphatic horizontal terminus to the "vertical walls." Finally, in 1949, when Wright published a memoir of his years with Sullivan, he said that the Wainwright Building had been "a splendid performance on the record for all time," but remarked that "the frontal divisions were still artificial." And he wrote that the picturesque verticality of the building "although appropriate, was still a mere façade."[16]

At last Wright acknowledged what he had been saying all along, that architecture ought to be conceived in three dimensions. Sullivan's preoccupation with the streetfront diminished the building art into a species of overscaled sculpture in relief, the very tradition Wright had deplored in his manifesto of 1901 as a superficial art "torn and hung upon the steel frame of commerce." In 1923, Wright again spoke to the issue:

> I am not of those who conceive a building as a carved and sculptured block of building material. That is two-dimension [sic] thinking. . . .
>
> The question I would ask concerning any architect or his building would be, is the architect's mind or is his work in two or in three dimensions? Is his work extraneous—applied from without, or an integral development from within?[17]

An architect committed to an integral development from within, as Wright meant to be, would not strive for emotional expression through a masonry cloak of ascribed symbolism. He would address the nature of the tall office building with its superimposed floors of rental space that cried out for daylight.

WRIGHT'S IDEA

In 1923, with little work and plenty of time, Wright pursued what he later called the "logical development of the idea of a tall building in the age of glass and steel." Glass, at last, would have its day. The drawings Wright produced in Los Angeles represented a breakthrough in his thinking. He intended to conceive the tall office building in a new spirit and he did. His idea of the skyscraper nevertheless remained a project in search of a client.[1]

At the end of November 1922, Wright had written Sullivan that he had "not a job in sight in the world," and might soon take leave of Taliesin "on the quest for work." He moved to Los Angeles by February 1923. His son Lloyd worked there, and so did R. M. Schindler, an emigré from Vienna. Both had worked for Wright on his buildings there for Aline Barnsdall. Schindler considered Los Angeles "the best city in the country for getting work," and Wright did secure a few commissions for houses, yet he was eager to undertake larger projects. With his dedication to the sovereignty of the individual and his extraordinary abilities in conceiving private houses as works of art, he seemed doomed to be regarded first and last as a residential architect. But he could not ignore the challenge of the most conspicuous and distinctive building type in America. The span of his life already had witnessed both the birth of the skyscraper and its proliferation. The skyscraper had become the architectural problem of the day. It had been Sullivan's principal field of endeavor, and now it engaged the imagination of architects everywhere.[2]

In June 1922, shortly before Wright returned to America from Japan, the *Chicago Tribune* announced an international design competition "to secure for Chicago the most beautiful office building in the world." The competition celebrated the newspaper's seventy-fifth anniversary. The most beautiful office building in the world was to rise 456 feet tall and become the paper's new administration building on Michigan Avenue. The competition ended that fall. It attracted more than 200 entries from architects in twenty-three countries. Many of the designs were sent on tour, and in May 1923—the date Wright inscribed on his skyscraper drawings in Los Angeles— eighty-five entries from the competition went on exhibit at the Art Institute of Chicago.[3]

Wright stood aloof from the *Tribune* competition. Juries inevitably chose the mediocre, he came to believe. ("What can a competition be," he wrote later, "except an averaging upon averages by the average?"). The first, second, and third prizes, respectively, went to John Mead Howells and Raymond Hood of New York, Eliel Saarinen of Helsinki, Finland, and Holabird & Roche of Chicago. To any modernist sensibility, the European entries far surpassed those from the United States. The most surprising—and finest—came not from Walter Gropius and Adolf Meyer in Germany, as so often averred, but from Bernard Bijvoet and Johannes Duiker of Holland. Inspired by the aesthetics of the movement known as "de Stijl," they envisioned a skyscraper with continuous bands of windows and with cantilevered floors, roofs, and sunshades. Clearly, they understood the great desideratum.[4]

Visionary projects for tall office buildings flourished in Europe in response to the dismal state of postwar life and the corresponding dearth of building activity. Erich Mendelsohn recalled many years later the urge "to work for the regeneration of our visual world, for the readjustment of our lives and habits to a new morality." He cited his own project of 1919 for a reinforced concrete skyscraper with "the whole structure and all the floors a cantilevered system." His idea nevertheless resided only in a quick perspective sketch, a tiny suggestion for a large building of rounded corners and great bands of glass, stepped back and upward as if a modern pyramid.[5]

The idea of the skyscraper proposed by Mies van der Rohe in two visionary projects of 1921–22 was more advanced; in each building the outer walls were to be entirely of glass. The structural system, although undefined, evidently would have relied on reinforced concrete mushroom columns and cantilevered floor slabs. Mies's spectacular concepts were published in Germany in 1922 but not in America until September 1923, the year the German architect and critic Walter Curt Behrendt praised various German projects for their development of "star-shaped" plans:

> The solution sought has been determined by the natural desire to facilitate as much as possible access of light and air to these giant structures. The

arrangement is that of wings projecting outward from the center of the block, permitting plenty of light and air to enter all rooms and therefore being especially advantageous for office buildings. Plans conceived according to this idea will, if highly developed, assume the shape of a star, stairways and elevators being arranged concentrically in the central part from which radiate the rather narrow wings with offices on both sides of an axial corridor.

By attending to purpose and structure, Behrendt wrote, German architects were discovering a new skyscraper form "independent of academic, classical traditions and expressive only by virtue of its own intrinsic character." He offered a critique of traditionalist American skyscrapers that applied equally well to Sullivan's formula:

> The architecture of the American skyscraper has closely followed the traditions established at the Ecole des Beaux Arts at Paris, utilizing the forms of decorative architectural expression in common usage, such as columns, pilasters, ornaments, et cetera. These great edifices thus frequently take the shape of enlarged Renaissance palaces, the three subdivisions of basement, superstructure and crowning cornice with attic, determining the scheme of the elevations. . . .[6]

Behrendt's essay appeared four months after Wright put onto paper his own new idea for the skyscraper. It demonstrated a parallel understanding of the importance of light, although in Europe visionary crystalline towers expressed in particular the will to purify and transform postwar society.[7]

In Los Angeles the immediate stimulus for Wright to design a skyscraper without any commission may well have come from his renewed contact with Schindler, who had first joined the Taliesin studio early in 1918. In July 1920, Richard Neutra wrote Schindler from Vienna asking for an account of American architecture, mentioning that Adolf Loos was at work on a row-house project that was to be "flanked by two skyscrapers." Schindler responded only after he arrived in Los Angeles in December 1920 to supervise Wright's buildings for Miss Barnsdall on Olive Hill. He wrote Neutra that Richardson's "large monumental square buildings" could be found in ugly American cities "like meteors from other planets." When he came to Sullivan, his comments sounded exactly like Wright's:

He was the first to proclaim "Form follows Function"

71. *Play Mart project, Los Angeles, rendering.*

and he tries to give the skyscraper a more appropriate form. He writes books on architecture for which no publisher can be found in America. His buildings represent the peak of the possible—for an architect who has not yet understood completely the third dimension and whose talent for beautiful ornamental sketches does not evoke a true feeling for materials.

Although he possessed an unbounded admiration for Wright's work, Schindler had a rare and attractive gift for fresh thinking, improvisation, and innovative techniques. His own double studio-house, designed and built in 1921–22 in West Hollywood, took form through the tilt-slab method of construction, which Irving Gill had used as early as 1913. The walls of reinforced concrete were cast in sections on the concrete floor, then lifted into place.[8]

Schindler conceived a radical skyscraper at least three months before Wright established his office on the West Coast. His preliminary drawings of the Play Mart, a project for the Frank Meline Company of Los Angeles, are dated October 1922 [71]. Schindler envisioned a glass elevator-tower flanked by office wings enclosed in black glass and aluminum. Such thin and light walls would have relied on floor slabs broadly cantilevered past their supports.[9]

Wright had romantically cantilevered the roofs of his prairie houses to express a comforting sense of shelter and the expansive space of the open landscape. But for the Imperial Hotel in Tokyo he had applied the cantilever principle to the floor slabs:

> . . . a construction was needed where floors would not be carried between walls because subterranean disturbances might move the walls and drop the floors.
>
> Why not then carry the floors as a waiter carries his tray on upraised arm and fingers at the center—*balancing* the load. All supports centered under the floor slabs like that instead of resting the slabs on the walls at their edges as is usually the case.
>
> This meant the cantilever, as I had found by now. The cantilever is most romantic—most free—of all principles of construction and in this case it seemed the most sensible.[10]

The hotel, damaged in the great earthquake of September 1, 1923, survived: a triumph, in Wright's mind, and a story he never tired of telling. The earthquake led him to denounce skyscrapers as agents of human sacrifice to greedy speculators and false civic pride; the Pacific Rim, he said, was no place to risk human life with the "architectural expedient" of the usual steel-frame building:

> Rigidity, it seems, was considered desirable by the skyscraper builders. A necessity it would be, in fact, to prevent the "architecture" from cracking and scaling from the skeletons. Yet tenuous flexibility is the chance for life of any sound construction in an earthquake—flexibility of foundation, flexibility of superstructure secured by continuous, lateral binding instruments from side to side in the floor planes of the structure, and the balancing of all loads well over vertical supporting members by means of the cantilever.[11]

The dynamics of the cantilever, Wright said, would outdistance ordinary skyscraper construction by exploring the third dimension and thus would represent "a development from within and not something merely applied from without." The cantilever principle would inspire a new expression in architecture. "We may now have release from time-honored platitudes," he wrote, "and try our wings with the 'flying slab.'"[12]

Wright first tried his wings with what he originally titled the "Commercial Building in Copper, Concrete and Glass" [72, 73]. Later he referred to the project as his "cantilever glass office building" or as "this structural idea for a skyscraper." He articulated the huge building by organizing it into a series of parallel fingers—the "four main transverse units"—extended perpendicular to a narrow spine that enclosed the elevators and principal corridor. The plan, extroverted and opposite to that of the Larkin Building, would not exactly accord with any of Behrendt's star-shaped varieties because the transverse units all reached in the same direction. In each, the most forward element was the stair tower, a fire escape. Wright left no trace of the traditional streetfront. Nor did he express the great vertical supports (enlarged and hollowed to carry the plumbing, heating, and electrical conduits) until the upper stories. His skyscraper was to be enclosed primarily with glass, the servant of light. Or, as he wrote:

> The exterior walls, as such, disappear—instead are suspended, standardized sheet-copper screens. The walls themselves cease to exist as either weight or thickness. Windows become in this fabrication a matter of a unit in the screen fabric, opening singly or in groups at the will of the occupant. All windows may

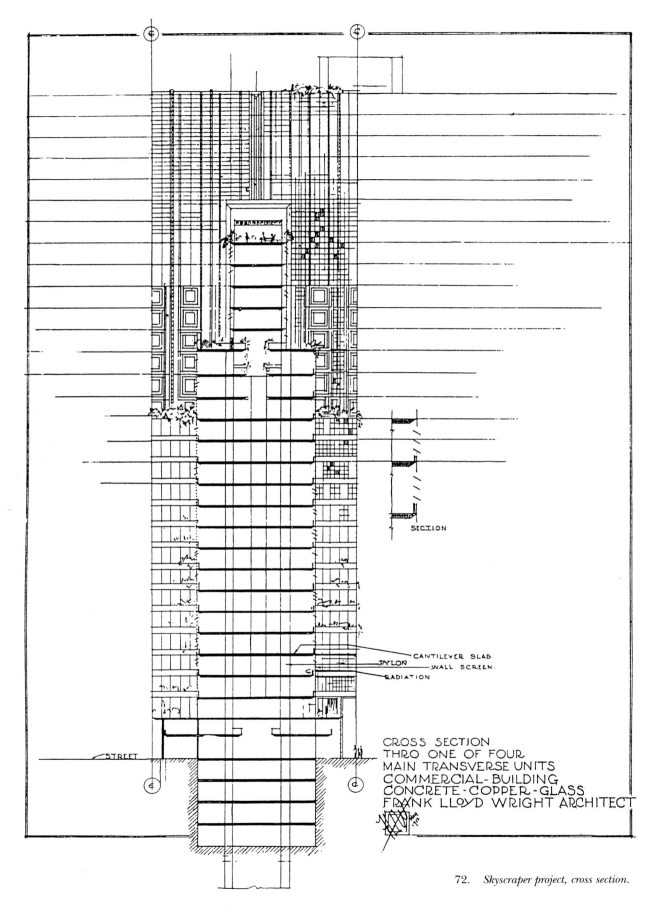

SECTION

CANTILEVER SLAB
PYLON
WALL SCREEN
RADIATION

CROSS SECTION
THRO ONE OF FOUR
MAIN TRANSVERSE UNITS
COMMERCIAL·BUILDING
CONCRETE·COPPER·GLASS
FRANK LLOYD WRIGHT ARCHITECT

STREET

72. *Skyscraper project, cross section.*

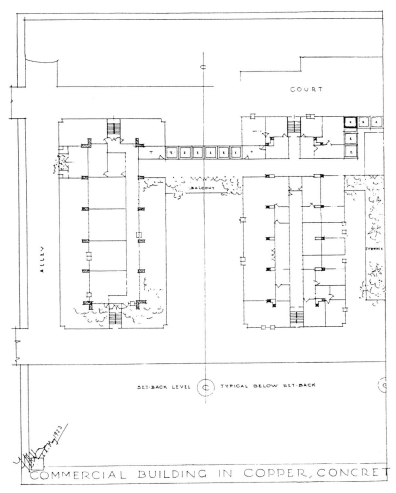

73. *Skyscraper project, half-plan.*

Once a precious substance limited in quantity and size, glass and its making have grown so that a perfect clarity of any thickness, quality or dimension is so cheap and desirable that our modern world is drifting toward structures of glass and steel.

The light-giving exterior screen, the vanished wall, and the new lightness and strength of construction made Wright's project a radical alternative to the type of skyscraper he had envisioned for the *Call*. In place of a clear-span tower configured as a narrow stockade of reinforced-concrete pilasters, he now imagined a fully articulated plan with a structure of cantilevered floor-slabs and comparatively few, but colossal, supports. That left the enclosure without any structural function—free to become a screen of glass held within a matrix of beautifully oxidized sheet-copper.[14]

Wright had achieved an idea of the skyscraper antithetical to Sullivan's. Its chief value, he wrote, resided in "the fact that the scheme as a whole legitimately eliminates the matter of masonry architecture that now vexes all such buildings." His glass skyscraper could easily serve as a prototype. Soon he began to daydream of a glass city:

> Imagine a city iridescent by day, luminous by night, imperishable! Buildings—shimmering fabrics—woven of rich glass—glass all clear or part opaque and part clear—patterned in color or stamped to form the metal tracery that is to hold all together to be, in itself, a thing of delicate beauty. . . . Such a city would clean itself in the rain, would know no fire alarms—nor any glooms. . . . The heating problem would be no greater than with the rattling windows of the imitation masonry structure, because the fabric now would be mechanically perfect—the product of the machine shop instead of the makeshift of the field.[15]

The mechanically perfect fabric was to consist of windows that closed tightly and copper mullions filled with insulation. Wright tended to specify details beyond the ordinary technology of the day, and he had always been overly sanguine about the thermal properties of glass. His prairie houses stretched into the landscape with long rows of casement windows and glass doors; the occupants suffered accordingly.

Thus the man who became Wright's client for the glass skyscraper may have had good reasons for not building it. Wright preferred to say he suffered from a lack of nerve. Albert M. Johnson had been president of the National Life Insurance Company since 1906, and his offices in

be cleaned from the inside with neither bother nor risk. The vertical mullions (copper shells filled with non-conducting material) are large and strong enough only to carry from floor to floor. . . . These protecting blades of copper act in the sun like the blades of a blind. . . .

Thus the outer building surfaces become opalescent, iridescent copper-bound glass. To avoid all interference with the fabrication of the light-giving exterior screen the supporting pylons are set back from the lot line, the floors carried by them thus becoming cantilever slabs . . . the construction being balanced as the body on the legs, the walls hanging as the arms from the shoulders. . . .[13]

Wright praised glass and light as two forms of the same thing. Modern machine-made glass, he said, would perhaps lead to the greatest differences between modern and ancient buildings:

74.   *National Life Insurance Company project, Chicago, rendering.*

Frank Lloyd Wright, Louis Sullivan and the Skyscraper

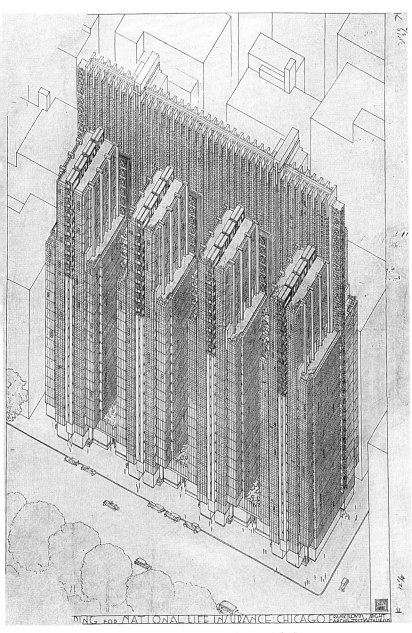

75. *National Life Insurance Company project, aerial view.*

Schindler wrote Neutra on February 2, 1924, that he could not say precisely how long Wright would remain in Los Angeles, but it seemed certain that he would "build a skyscraper in Chicago, and in any case his office will be in Chicago." Neutra already was enamored of Wright's architecture without having seen it, and he decided to leave New York for the Midwest. He met Wright for the first time on April 16, at the funeral of Louis Sullivan.[17]

Wright by then was making plans for an irrigated desert compound for Johnson and his chum Scotty near the northern end of Death Valley, California. The prospect of building a remote residential compound near an imaginary gold mine, of course, could not begin to compare with even the slightest chance of building a glass skyscraper facing Water Tower Square in Chicago. Neutra's wife, Dione, nevertheless struggled to understand how much the skyscraper project meant to Wright. When she wrote her parents in July 1924, she expressed dismay over his manner at Taliesin:

> A big industrialist with wife, daughter, and son-in-law were houseguests, and it was to be decided whether Wright would be commissioned to build a skyscraper. All his hopes were based on this. For weeks all had been prepared for this visit. The office had been enlarged, an annex added for twenty draftsmen. . . .
>
> We were introduced. Mr. Johnson is an elderly, harmless, benevolent, little, dull-looking man. One would never suspect him to be a millionaire. . . . Wright sat in an easy chair. It was somewhat painful for us to see such an outstanding man humbling himself by being amiable, offering hospitality in order to get a commission. . . . He sits without work on his wonderful estate, carrying innumerable construction ideas in his mind; probably too beautiful to fit into our world.[18]

By being amiable, Wright at least succeeded; Johnson returned to Chicago and on July 19 wrote him:

> I shall be very glad to hear from you as to what progress you are making, as I am intensely interested and everything seems to indicate that Upper Michigan Avenue is going ahead very rapidly, even more so than some of us anticipated.

It was clear from Johnson's letter that he regarded the project as real-estate speculation. He asked Wright to make preliminary studies for a building of "undetermined height and undetermined cost" on all or part of a

Chicago were at 29 South La Salle Street, in a building designed by William Le Baron Jenney and William B. Mundie. He had in mind for the glass skyscraper a magnificent site that looked directly south to the Water Tower, the most beloved landmark in the city.[16] A wealthy man, Johnson seemed generous to a fault. For decades, and to no end except his own amusement, he financed Walter Scott, the notorious flimflam man known as Death Valley Scotty. An inveterate stuntsman and publicity seeker, Scotty pretended to be working a hidden gold mine. Johnson himself, curiously, had once been a miner—but in Joplin, Missouri, and for lead and zinc.

site between Pearson and Chestnut streets and from Michigan Avenue on the east to the Quigley Memorial Seminary on the west. (The seminary had been built in 1917–18 in a Gothic style; its chapel, at the northeast corner of Rush and Pearson streets, was inspired by the Sainte-Chapelle in Paris.) Wright was to be paid $20,000 for plans drawn to one-eighth-inch scale, perhaps a model, and such other studies as would represent an "exhaustive analysis" of all the practical details of the glass skyscraper. The building might be constructed in sections, Johnson wrote, a possibility he may have found implicit in the "four main transverse units" shown in Wright's drawings from the year before.

The project at Water Tower Square, Wright said, gave him "an opportunity to devise a more practical solution of the skyscraper problem than current" [74, 75]. He planned to exploit the entire site:

> To gratify Mr. Johnson, the landlord, his lot area was now salable to the very lot-line itself and on every floor, where ordinances do not interfere and demand that they be reduced in area as the building soars.

What architecture there is in evidence here is a light, trim, practical, commercial fabric—every inch and pound of which is "in service." There is every reason why it should be beautiful.

Hence he argued that the skyscraper problem could best be solved by wholeheartedly accepting the commercial conditions and purposes of the building. Again the "thin pendent wall-screens" were to be of sheet-copper and glass:

> . . . and to avoid the prejudice I saw in my client's mind against excessive glass surfaces I decided to make the exterior area of this project about ¼ of copper and ¾ of glass. . . . The unit of two feet both ways is small because of Mr. Johnson's fear of "too much glass."[19]

But in fact Wright had adopted the small unit or module in his scheme of 1923, and it more essentially expressed his own desire to break down the enormous dimensions of the tall office building into details of a human and intimate scale. An enclosure three-fourths of

76. *National Life Insurance Company project, interior perspective.*

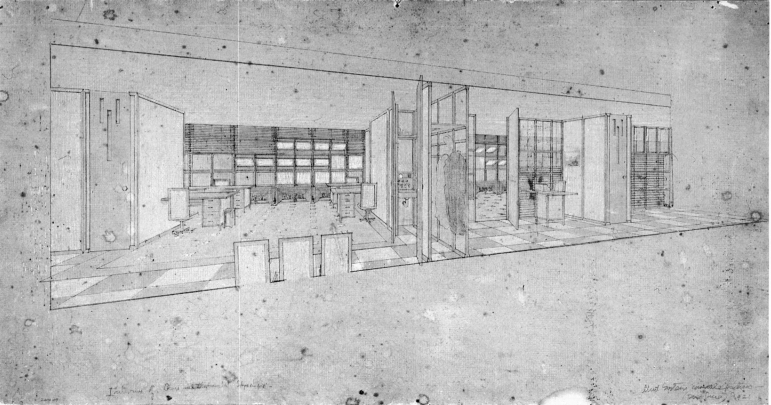

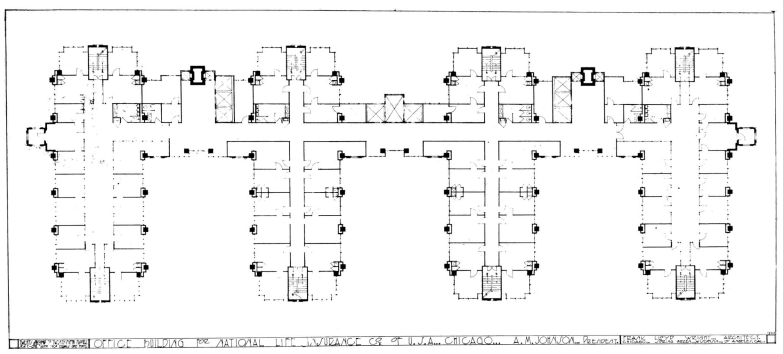

77. *National Life Insurance Company project, plan of 22nd to 25th floors.*

glass, moreover, would more than double the ratio of glass to opaque surfaces in the streetfronts of the Wainwright Building.

The small window units and blinds could easily be adjusted for the desired amount of light and ventilation [76]. Wright's interior studies also illustrated a fully modular system for office arrangements:

> Being likewise fabricated on a perfect unit system, the interior-partitions may all be made up in sections, complete with doors, ready to set in place, and designed to match the general style of the outer wall-screen.
>
> These interior partition units thus fabricated may be stored ready to use, and any changes to suit ten-

ants made overnight with no waste of time and material. Mr. Johnson was an experienced landlord and all this simplicity appealed to him. Again the kind of standardization that gives us the motor car.[20]

The plan for the setback stories, much improved from the scheme of 1923, now provided more than twice as many offices [77]. Sixteen of them were corner offices, and by contrast to those of the Wainwright Building were to be enclosed entirely with glass.

Wright continued his studies into 1925. He engaged Charles Morgan, an architect known for his flair in making perspective drawings, to prepare a series of breathtaking renderings. The drawings may have appealed to Johnson, but he never carried the project forward.[21]

78. *St. Mark's Tower project, New York.*

THE ANTI-SKYSCRAPER

Impelled by his "structural idea for a skyscraper," Wright soon envisioned a tall building of more dynamic form. Now he proposed a slender and small-scale tower standing free in a parklike setting. Quadruple in plan, enclosed only with copper and glass, the tower would attend in every way to the changing light of day. It would rise like a tall tree, a splendid incident upon the landscape. The project for St. Mark's Tower became the prototype Wright never let die [78].

Whenever it was that he first imagined the tower, Wright waited until the end of 1928 before he made the preliminary drawings. His friend William Norman Guthrie, rector of St. Mark's in-the-Bouwerie, in New York, had been thinking of a tall apartment building that could generate more income for the church. A kindred soul, Guthrie was a native of Scotland and nearly Wright's age. Although his stone church had stood since 1799 on what had been "the Bouwerie," or farm, of Peter Stuyvesant, the last Dutch governor-general in America, Guthrie himself was known as a flamboyantly unorthodox Episcopal clergyman. "To do anything in St. Mark's meant to become an ecclesiastical outlaw," he wrote Wright in 1914. "I couldn't be elected to [a] rat-hole anywhere else." Guthrie also wrote that he deemed Wright one of the two most "interesting & irritating" persons he had ever met.[1]

Guthrie had put Wright to work as early as 1908 on plans for a house in Sewanee, Tennessee, where he was then teaching literature at the University of the South. He eventually decided against building and even against teaching. In 1909 he lectured at the University of Chicago, but the next year he accepted the call to St. Mark's. Wright said he could never think of Guthrie "otherwise than in a fervor over some quest, spiritual or aesthetic." Indeed, the rector of St. Mark's once took pains to correct Wright on the nature and functions of the ancient Greek temple, and on another occasion wrote of refreshing himself by reading Bernard Bosanquet's *History of Aesthetic* as well as writings by George Santayana and Vernon Lee. Although Guthrie never built anything he asked Wright to design, he surely ranked as one of Wright's most intelligent and formidable clients.[2]

As a man of letters, Guthrie took a paradoxical interest in ways of nonverbal communication. His mission, he told Wright, was nothing less than the "reconstruction of religious expression to make religion again sincerely possible." This meant brave new rituals in sound, color, procession, and dance, even "vast sacramental visions [set] to music—with movement." Calvinism, he asserted, had "starved the beauty of the church service" and killed Protestantism. "My brain dances," Guthrie once wrote Wright, "& I've planned out so many new rituals my choirmaster is having a picnic."[3]

Wright entertained grand visions of his own. Sometimes he indulged in a paper-architecture of the kind he professed to disdain. Early in 1926 he sketched a great openwork steel-and-glass canopy, tripodal in structure, for a "Commercial Arts Festival." It was to rise 1,360 feet, taller than the Eiffel Tower (which he lightly drew alongside it, for convenient comparison) and more than eight times taller than the vault of the Cathedral of Beauvais, the tallest in French Gothic architecture. In a note on the drawing, Wright said the tripodal structure was to have a "central chamber stepped down to great 'Fountain of Elements' to form vast audience hall seating 100,000 people." When asked by Guthrie to conceive a colossal interfaith cathedral, he simply made a few revisions in the fantasy project for the huge canopy.[4]

Small wonder that a mind so nimble as Wright's would become engaged in pipe dreams when no work was at hand. Unemployed, however, Wright held his head even higher, a posture that could not pass unnoticed. Guthrie too was theatrical, but he had a more practical side. St. Mark's needed to address its financial crisis, he said, either by launching an endowment campaign for $1 million or by constructing a tall apartment building near the church. On October 19, 1927, he wrote Wright that he preferred to build. But he warned:

> I have had long and perfectly frank consultations. I can get my project through properly without friction provided I give you up. You are not "persona grata" and I have got a nice job now to tell you why without losing your friendship.

You blow in breezily, assume everybody knows you are the greatest architect in the world. . . . You appear . . . egotistical, overbearing, arrogant.

Of course, if we undertake the building we propose, there are architects in New York standing in line . . . who are all equally good, as they can give equally good references for integrity, efficiency and business backing. Any man who has put up a skyscraper is better than you who haven't put up any. What guarantee have we that you can put up a good skyscraper? We can't afford a mistake. . . .

A design proposal from a New York architect, Guthrie wrote, would cost the church about $150. Wright answered on October 26:

It would be foolish indeed to argue my case. . . . You have load enough to carry without me.

And yet I think, being as you say "egotistical, overbearing and arrogant," that I could make the project live as no other architect would—even if he could.

But I do suffer from all the handicaps you mention—including ideas. . . .

There is no sacrifice I would not make to help your cause forward—you know me well enough for that I hope.

But, when you talk of a $150.00 sketch, you show to what extent do you know nothing at all about intensive organic effort in architecture such as mine. . . .

My work must be substantially done before you can see how it will look—hence the real difficulty in this case.

Later, he grew more specific in a memorandum he wrote in New York and left undated:

As you know, I have been working many years on a simplification of the modern building problem looking toward permanence also. The Imperial Hotel was a proof of my success. Another preliminary study for a tall building for the National Life Insurance Co. of Chicago for which they paid me $25,000.00 [sic] carried it to the point where costs and details to the minute points of construction are well in hand. I may say construction is now ⅓ lighter and three times stronger than anything yet built. And there is a saving in floor area of about 15% in a twelve-story building, more as the building goes higher. . . . There is the added strength, the added floor space and the element of permanence (such a building needs no

amortization in less than a century) and of inward beauty owing to simplicity and integrity.

For plans, perspectives and detail drawings sufficient for "tentative estimates" of construction costs, Wright asked $7,500, not $150. Guthrie nevertheless continued to plead for a simple picture to show the vestry. In an undated letter, he told Wright:

You always play *solitaire*. That's our difficulty. . . . Only genius condescending to magic can save us—coercing, bamboozling them with pictures. That you can't give them. . . . All they want is a picture that "gets" them. They must see an *idol*—an outside. . . . And you want to develop a perfectly realizable organic plan. O dear theorist—you talk as a Moses just back from Sinai. What they want is a Peter Pan.

A year later, Guthrie still was asking for a picture "such as is displayed in our Architectural League annual exhibitions." In a letter of November 12, 1928, he outlined the financial conditions that controlled any apartment project. Renters much preferred addresses near Fifth Avenue, he said. So far as Tenth Street, the block between Fourth and Third avenues was deplorable, and although St. Mark's had improved the properties it already owned between Third and Second avenues, the problem was how to gain "*enough prestige* to interest renters—when they are 'shopping' (because of overbuilding & vacancies) so that we can make them jump over a bad block." He continued:

Finance people usually dictate the architect. That's the trouble in New York. Do you apprehend? . . .

What chance have I commending you with no sketch—no proposition—against some architect who points to what he has actually *erected* in Manhattan? . . .

The bank is the master. Next the building company. Next the architect. That's our hierarchy. Please do not imagine I like this. I'm a professional & don't like to see my class set down as *third*, but I see they are. In the university world it's the same.

So long as he could take charge of design, Wright offered to associate with a New York architect. Finally, as the year was about to end, he sat down to make sketches. Donald Walker, who had joined the Taliesin studio in October, recalled many years later that it was on Christmas Day of 1928 that Wright made the first drawings for St. Mark's:

Mr. Wright entered the studio (I was alone) and asked me to put some paper on his board. I stood by, watching for four hours, until he put his pencil down and said, "Don, that is architecture. Make me some working drawings."[5]

Wright and his entourage soon left for Arizona, and near Chandler they built a temporary camp he named "Ocatilla." They spent about four months on the working drawings for San Marcos in the Desert, a resort hotel destined never to be built. From the desert camp Wright wrote Guthrie on March 4, 1929, that he had "already made sketches" for St. Mark's Tower. By the time Wright next visited New York, several months later, Guthrie had

left for four months of traveling through Europe. "When you return," Wright wrote him on August 6, "we shall have something tangible for you to center your imagination on. We have here a really great project in every sense."

Although the rector had gone abroad, Wright felt free to meet with the chairman of the finance committee, and in October, after Guthrie had returned, he met with two other vestrymen as well. One was Warren Shepard Matthews, an architectural engineer, who soon sent Wright a plot plan of the properties surrounding the church and its cemetery.

A vintage real estate map illustrates what St. Mark's owned by the end of 1929, as well as the angled orientation of the church [79]. Immediately west of the church

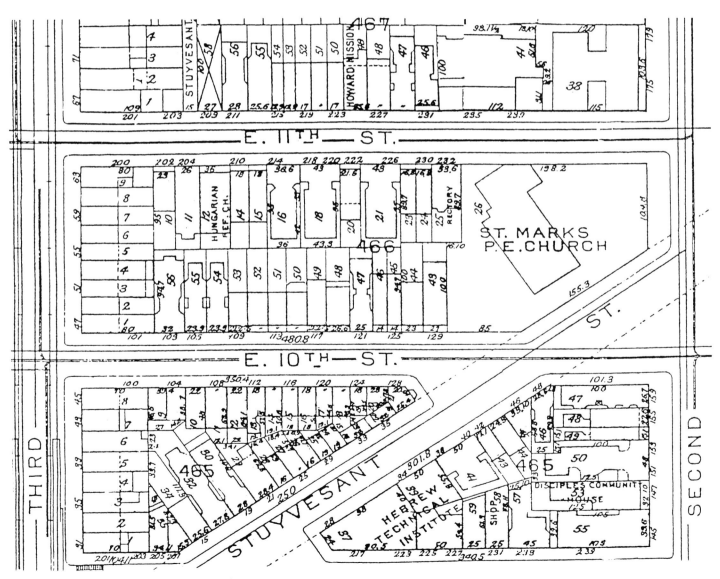

79.   *Real estate map, St. Mark's neighborhood.*

80. *St. Mark's Tower project, rendering.*

grounds, St. Mark's owned all but one of the buildings from 109 through 129 East Tenth Street; if the church could acquire the six-story tenement at 121 East Tenth, it would control a 240-foot frontage facing south. The church also owned the rectory at 232–34 East Eleventh Street and the two narrow houses next to it. In proposing a series of purchases to the west, the properties committee hoped to assemble a 211-foot frontage facing north on Eleventh Street. Finally, the church owned four buildings at what was known as the gore of Stuyvesant and

Tenth streets: 126 and 128 East Tenth and 33 and 35 Stuyvesant. The gore was the first site proposed for St. Mark's Tower.[6]

Wright boldly suggested that each successful tower could easily finance the building of another [80, 81]. He wrote Matthews on October 30, 1929, that the first tower should stand near the church:

I should like to see more of a park-like aspect about the base of the building than would be possible on

IN THE BOUWERIE, NEW YORK CITY FRANK LLOYD WRIGHT ARCHITECT

81. *St. Mark's Tower project, aerial perspective.*

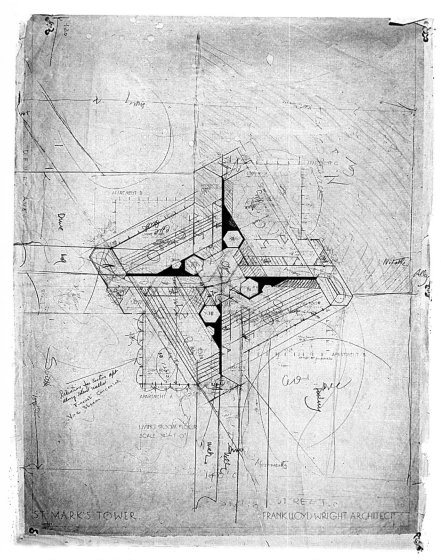

82. *St. Mark's Tower project, plan, with changes in 1952.*

responded specifically and immediately to the angled siting of the church itself and to the energetic intersection of Stuyvesant Street with Tenth Street, which produced nearly a 30-degree angle [82].

To meet the building code, Wright prepared drawings of towers from twelve to twenty stories tall. Essentially, however, he envisioned for St. Mark's a tower of eighteen stories above a narrowed entrance pedestal [83]. The tower would grow wider as it rose higher, he explained:

> The building increases substantially in area from floor to floor as the structure rises—in order that the glass frontage of each story may drip clear of the one below, the building, thus, cleaning itself, and, also

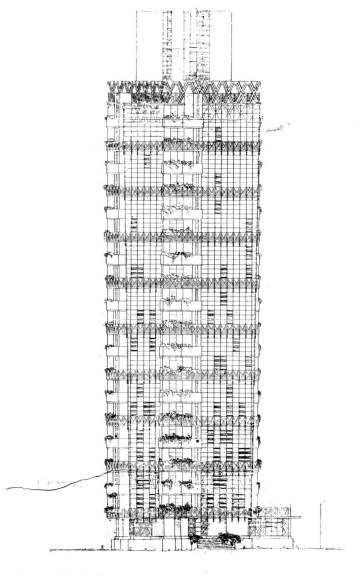

83. *St. Mark's Tower project, elevation.*

the detached triangle [the gore] unless we acquired one more lot to the rear extending from street to street. Also, I believe the relationship between the old church and the modern prismatic-building would be extremely agreeable.

Wright's idea of the "modern prismatic-building" carried forward the theme of his Luxfer Prism project from more than thirty years earlier. The prismatic quality, no longer limited to a front composed of glass blocks, now suffused the entire structure. In the design of the Ocatilla camp and the project for San Marcos in the Desert he had played with reflexive configurations of 30–60 degree angles, or what he called the one-two triangle. But now the same angles in the prismatic plan for St. Mark's Tower

84. *St. Mark's Tower project, cutaway perspective of interior.*

because areas become more valuable the higher (within limits) the structure goes.

The eighteen-story version would offer thirty-six duplex apartments, four on every other floor, or thirty-two rental units if the rectory occupied the top floors. Each apartment would feature a two-story studio living room with a dining area and adjacent kitchenette [84]. Wright intended the furniture and partitions to be of metal, as in the National Life Insurance Company project. Two bedrooms would be offered on the mezzanine or balcony floor, angled at 30 degrees from the principal face of the living room [85]. A series of interior windows would give onto the upper part of the living room, and both levels would open to small outdoor balconies.[7]

Wright said St. Mark's Tower expressed "interior space in light," because light inspired nearly every aspect of the "modern prismatic-building": the plan, structural system, elevations and siting. Much earlier, he had thought of the Larkin Building plan as "systematically quartered" and centered on the internal light court. The building was

85. *St. Mark's Tower project, cutaway perspective of bedroom mezzanine.*

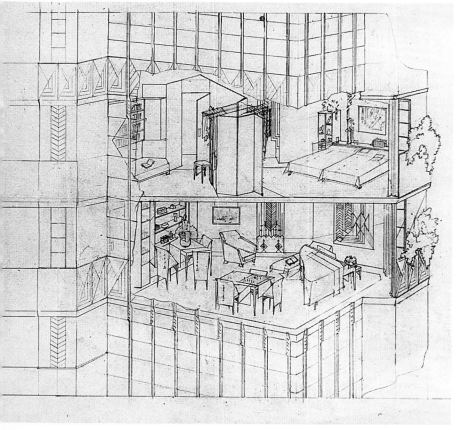

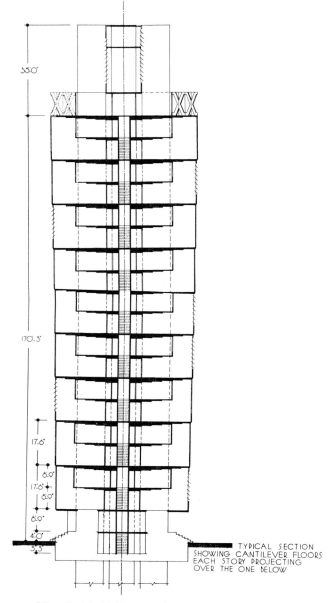

TYPICAL SECTION
SHOWING CANTILEVER FLOORS
EACH STORY PROJECTING
OVER THE ONE BELOW

86. *St. Mark's Tower project, section.*

consciously introverted, and the plan—except for the rifts that defined the stair towers—remained static. But in St. Mark's Tower the quartered or quadruple plan arose from the pinwheel of four great interior supports in reinforced concrete. Wright meant to eliminate all "outer masonry walls and interior partitions." His plan spun the living areas outward and to the light.[8]

The bladelike supports, he emphasized, would stand "inside away from lighted space" [86]. To the same end, in his prairie houses so many years earlier, he had situated the masonry fireplace masses as far as possible from the casement windows and French doors. The cantilevered floor slabs of St. Mark's Tower, moreover, were to be progressively diminished to a section of only 3 inches at the perimeter: Lightness of structure was to admit more light for living. Finally, the tower would stand free, surrounded by greenery and open to the grace of sunlight. Its copper fins would modulate the light and create ever-changing patterns of sun and shadow. Even when Wright discussed the sheet-metal partitions and furniture, he asserted that "the equivalent of a five-room apartment, cave style, may be had in two-thirds of the space. Sunlight method."[9]

But the idea of a skyscraper apartment tower "in which all construction is removed to the interior . . . the outer walls becoming mere window screens," failed to take hold at St. Mark's. Wright went East in May 1930 to give a series of lectures at Princeton University, and at last attended a formal meeting of the vestry in New York. The most compelling objections to the tower came from a vestryman who was a real estate lawyer. In a letter of May 20, Guthrie recapitulated:

> That was a body blow we received from Justin Miner. We are obviously down and out . . . we cannot possibly build anything that has not definite precedents from which positively accurate estimates of cost can be made. . . . This, as you see, makes any adventures in architectural structure hopelessly out of the question.
>
> When I first started my day-dreaming, it was because I believed so deeply in beauty; but I was not prepared, of course, for the terrible factual revelations of Mr. Miner. . . . We don't really need originality. What we must really have in our plan is financial acceptability, to allow us as a corporation to proceed. . . .

A few weeks later, on June 9, Guthrie wrote Wright again:

> The more I think of the tower, the more convinced I am that it should not be in the city at all, but in a grove of trees full of brown thrashers or mockingbirds. . . . Being open to a friendly world is one thing, and being in our style world, in which one seeks refuge, is another. . . . I fancy after all that this tower is the creature of the Taliesin world, where to be open to all that is goodly and Godly is the supreme craving of the soul. You ridicule the cave, but I suspect that in Manhattan each has to have a cave in which he can escape sight and sound and the new detective systems by which privacy is abolished, and one dreams of a primal cave very much in the heart

of a mountain. . . . After all, if you wish to give people shelter, you must know what their enemies are, and share their life of self-defence.[10]

Wright nevertheless kept his "sunlight method" alive by trying to get the tower built elsewhere in New York, Chicago, or Detroit. "You yourself do not know yet what the thing is all about," he wrote Guthrie on February 9, 1931. "You've been poisoned by the New York atmosphere."

Who could have dreamed that the tower someday would be built in a place so remote as Bartlesville, Oklahoma, and on a site that hardly called out for a tall building? Such were the facts, however, that served Wright perfectly. When asked to design an office building of only three stories, he chose instead to rekindle the idea of St. Mark's Tower. Now he could prove that it was possible to change both the scale and the value of a most recalcitrant architectural type, the skyscraper.

Reborn as the Price Tower, his skyscraper celebrated light as the great desideratum and as the great source of life and beauty. Wright described it as a "light-fabric," a work dedicated to "the value of sunlit space." It championed the release of the tall building, he said, from "congested areas of monstrous cities" to a typical "country town." And it showed how the tall building might become intrinsically desirable, a much finer thing than a mere engine of profit. Wright set out to transform the skyscraper in a substantive way, not by ascribing to it an esoteric symbolic content. When he talked about a tree that escaped the crowded forest, the metaphor struck true because it inhered in the very structure of his tall, solitary tower [87, 88].[11]

Harold C. Price became the patron for Wright's noble anti-skyscraper. He operated an international pipeline company, needed little office space for his headquarters in Bartlesville, and had no desire to build a corporate symbol of any advertising value. Price in fact preferred buildings low to the ground, and particularly admired the work of Clifford May, pioneer of the California ranch house. Early in 1952 he was thinking about a new headquarters:

> We wanted a building of our own. We agreed to build a three story building with another company taking the entire first floor. My two sons, Harold and Joe, recently graduated from the University of Oklahoma, suggested we get Frank Lloyd Wright to design the building. . . . However, I did not believe that Mr. Wright would be interested in such a small building.

87.   *Price Tower, Bartlesville, Oklahoma, perspective study.*

Wright indeed was not. Price's two sons had suggested Wright at the recommendation of Bruce Goff, then chairman of the school of architecture at the University of Oklahoma, in Norman. As recalled by Harold C. Price, Jr.:

> Joe had somehow met Bruce Goff. . . . So, Dad gave Joe the assignment of talking to Bruce about who we should get. . . . Bruce told Joe that he'd like to do the building himself, but if we really wanted the best architect in the United States we ought to get Frank Lloyd Wright.

An act of great generosity was repaid in a most mean-spirited way; several years later, Wright undermined the plans Goff had drawn for a bachelor's studio-house for Joe Price.[12]

Harold C. Price and his family flew to Wisconsin in June 1952 to meet with Wright. "I told him I wanted a three story building with about 25,000 square feet of floor space," Price recalled. "He said immediately that three floors was most inefficient and suggested ten floors of 2,500 square feet each." Wright was offering the smallest version of the project for St. Mark's, a fact that may have

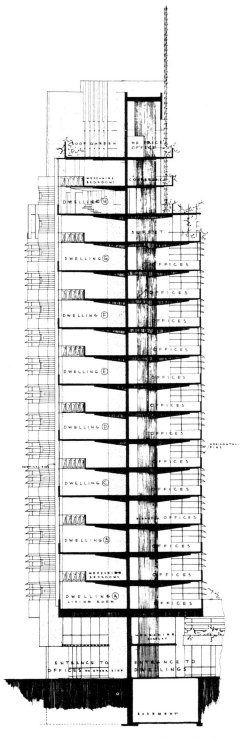

88. *Price Tower, section through south side.*

89. *Site preparation for Price Tower, looking northeast.*

Three stories of the tower would be occupied by his own company, he wrote, and the first floor and one or two more would be rented to the Public Service Company of Oklahoma. Price had acquired a site measuring 140 by 150 feet at the northeast corner of Sixth Street and Dewey Avenue, not far from the center of downtown Bartlesville [89].[13]

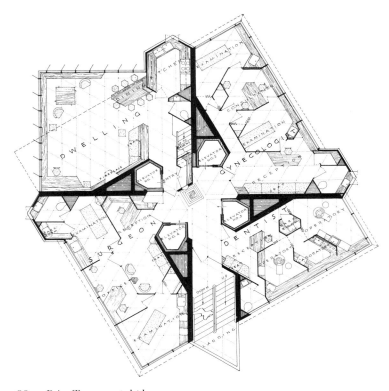

90. *Price Tower, rental plan.*

come to Price's attention then or soon after. Price wrote on August 19 that he had revised his program to "a building of no less than ten stories." He also told Wright there was a demand in Bartlesville for "what might be called deluxe apartments" with two bedrooms and two baths.

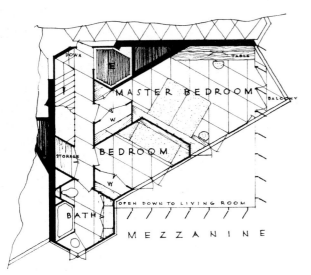

91. *Price Tower, plan of bedroom mezzanine.*

92. *Price Tower, elevator.*

93. *Price Tower, hall and entry to office.*

Everything went Wright's way. In one quadrant of the tower he could at last realize the duplex apartment plan he had conceived for St. Mark's [90, 91]. He began the design of the Price Tower in August, and the working drawings date from the winter of 1952–53. The building was finished early in 1956. Price expected to spend $500,000, and at first Wright assured him the costs would run only $18 to $20 a square foot. But by April 1953 Wright was assuming a "cost price of about a million." Later, the budget was set at $1.25 million. In the end, Price wrote on August 30, 1956, the tower had cost $52 a square foot, or about $2.1 million. Apart from the tower, Price and his elder son had asked Wright to design houses—one in Paradise Valley, Arizona, and the other in Bartlesville. "The cost of the Tower and the two houses," Price wrote Wright, "has placed an embarrassing strain on both the company and the family." Even if the tower could be fully rented, he noted, it would generate a gross profit of only $24,000 a year: a return of little more than one percent, not including depreciation.

Because he had virtually eliminated the original purpose of a tall office building, Wright courted a certain irony when he spoke of "this release of the skyscraper from slavery (of commercial bondage) to a human freedom."[14]

The values Wright asserted when he described the Price Tower obviously diverged from those of the business world:

> . . . preferred, convenient, compact space in open sky—fresh air and far views . . . its spaces commanding the wonders of light and sky over the rolling plains of Oklahoma . . . a splendid isolation . . .

The tower did not offer normal office spaces, and the "deluxe" apartments Price had requested—although literally "of the light"—were hardly suited to family life. The intricacies of the building, and its surprising intimacies of scale, could be sensed immediately in the elevations and on the way to the interior suites [92, 93]. From a plan only 46 feet wide the building broke down into quadrants and then to a unit or module shaped as a rhombus composed of two equilateral triangles. The unit related to the dynamic rotation in the plan, but its dimension of only 2 feet 10⅝ inches on each side made a most eccentric module of construction. Curtis Besinger has recalled:

> The parallel lines of the unit were thirty inches apart. In doing the developmental drawings, those of us who were assisting Mr. Wright questioned this

94. *Price Tower, office quadrants and fire escape, looking west.*

dimension. . . . We proposed that it should be a little larger, that it was too small for a public building. The unit system being used made many situations in the plan somewhat tight and cramped. He rejected our proposal and insisted that the tower was to be tall and slender.

Because unit-lines determined the partitions and the placement of various items of furniture, the interior space gained fresh but sometimes awkward configurations. The

95. *Price Tower, office quadrants and light-needle, looking southwest.*

96. *Price Tower, office interior.*

97.   *Price Tower, apartment living room.*

98. *Price Tower, apartment dining area.*

99. *Price Tower, bedroom and balcony.*

division of the narrow tower into quadrants, moreover, deprived it of the flexibility Wright had proposed so convincingly in his drawings for the National Life Insurance Company project.[15]

The Price Tower stood nineteen stories and about 190 feet tall. Day and night it played with light [94, 95]. It also admitted more light than could be successfully controlled by the gold-tinted glass and the copper fins or blades—nearly all fixed—meant to serve as sunscreens [96]. But the lovely verdigris of the copper, which appeared as well in the fascia panels, greatly contributed to the character of the tower. The panels were stamped with a complex pattern inspired by that of the floor plan.[16]

From his unequaled feeling for an intimate and yet noble scale, Wright was able to give the Price Tower the same aura of human dignity and potentiality that pervaded the best of his houses [97–99]. He demanded an order of architecture quite beyond the inert and uninflected spaces of the typical tall office building. Little wonder that he failed to become a successful architect of skyscrapers. He nonetheless drove to the heart of the problem and opened the walls to the light of day. William Norman Guthrie was right when he saw in the project for St. Mark's a creature of the Taliesin world, "open to all that is good and Godly." Wright finally brought to a small town of the Midwest a tall building conceived in a new spirit and thereby endowed with the true strangeness of beauty [100].

100. *Price Tower, apartment quadrant, looking predominantly east.*

NOTES

Notes—Introduction

1. Claude Bragdon, "Letters from Louis Sullivan," *Architecture* LXIV (July 1931), p. 9; Bragdon, *More Lives Than One* (New York, 1938), p. 157; Louis H. Sullivan, *The Autobiography of an Idea* [1924] (Dover reprint, New York, 1956), pp. 298, 314; and Sullivan, "The Tall Office Building Artistically Considered," *Lippincott's* LVII (March 1896), p. 406.

Sullivan's friend and mentor John Edelmann pronounced the Wainwright Building "the most complete expression of American commercial architecture" even before construction was finished; see his essay on "Pessimism of Modern Architecture," *Engineering Magazine* III (April 1892), p. 47.

Many standard studies merely repeat Sullivan's self-congratulation and thus give to his hyperbole an artificial patina of historical fact.

Notes—The Engine of Profit

1. Louis H. Sullivan, "Development of Building—II," the *Economist* (Chicago) LVI (July 1, 1916), p. 40. Hale had previously manufactured hydraulic elevators. Aldis was a lawyer. For the Reliance Building, see my study *The Architecture of John Wellborn Root* (Chicago, 1988), pp. 177–91.

2. Sullivan, "What Is Architecture," in *Kindergarten Chats* [1918] *and Other Writings* (Dover reprint, New York, 1979), p. 232. Wright referred to Adler as the "chief" and to Sullivan as "lieber Meister." He proudly recalled preparing the office plan for publication; it appeared the day before his twenty-third birthday, in the *Engineering and Building Record* XXII (June 7, 1890), p. 5. The same journal had published Burnham & Root's office plan five months earlier, as the first in a series on "The Organization of the Architect's Office." The studio addition Wright built at his home in Oak Park, Ill., in 1898 also featured a two-story drafting room. For his memoir *Genius and the Mobocracy,* published in 1949, Wright had the Adler & Sullivan office plan redrawn, and he did not include the balcony plan.

3. Sullivan, *The Autobiography of an Idea,* pp. 292, 288–89, and "The Tall Office Building Artistically Considered," p. 403.

4. The *Economist* V (May 30, 1891), p. 951, and Dankmar Adler, "Tall Office Buildings—Past and Future," *Engineering Magazine* III (Sept. 1892), pp. 766–67. Adler elsewhere characterized the new building type as the "sky-scraping temple of Mammon"; see *Chicago Tribune,* Oct. 29, 1893, p. 37.

5. *Chicago Tribune,* Nov. 30, 1890, p. 28, and *St. Louis Post-Dispatch,* Oct. 28, 1890, p. 2.

6. The *Times* (Chicago), Feb. 21, 1885, p. 6. The *Tribune* of the same day, p. 2, said Amos Grannis spent about $130,000 in building the block and sold it less than four months before the fire to Shepherd Brooks of Boston for $185,000.

7. *Chicago Tribune,* Jan. 13, 1889, p. 2.

8. *Chicago Tribune,* Sept. 13, 1891, p. 25.

9. *The Meanings of Architecture: Buildings and Writings by John Wellborn Root,* ed. Donald Hoffmann (New York, 1967), p. 134.

10. Sullivan, "The Tall Office Building Artistically Considered," pp. 405–6; A. D. F. Hamlin, *History of Architecture* (New York, 1896), p. 396; Barr Ferree, "The High Building and Its Art," *Scribner's Magazine* XV (March 1894), pp. 314, 312, 303, 300, and Sullivan, ibid., p. 406.

"The economic height is that above which each added story constitutes a bad investment of the capital required for its construction," Francisco Mujica noted in his *History of the Skyscraper* (New York, 1930), p. 21. The degree to which real estate speculation created downtown Chicago is made particularly clear by Gerald R. Larson in "Chicago's Loop, 1830–1890: A Tale of Two Grids," in *Fragments of Chicago's Past* (Chicago, 1990), pp. 68–79. Carol Willis writes of the "awesome effects of the profit motive" in "Light, Height, and Site: The Skyscraper in Chicago," in *Chicago Architecture and Design 1923–1993,* ed. John Zukowsky (Munich, 1993), p. 119, and in her study *Form Follows Finance* (New York, 1995), pp. 181–82, declares: "The first blueprint for every tall building is a balance sheet of estimated costs and returns."

For the history of early tall buildings in New York, see Sarah Bradford Landau and Carl W. Condit, *Rise of the New York Skyscraper 1865–1913* (New Haven, Ct., 1996).

11. "What Is Architecture?: A Study in the American People of Today" [1906], in *Louis Sullivan: The Public Papers,* ed. Robert Twombly (Chicago, 1988), p. 175; *Kindergarten Chats,* p. 78; and "The Tall Office Building Artistically Considered," pp. 403, 406.

12. *Civilizing American Cities: A Selection of Frederick Law Olmsted's Writings on City Landscapes,* ed. S. B. Sutton (Cambridge, Mass., 1971), pp. 18–19, and R. Kerr, "On the Lofty Buildings of New York City," *Sanitary Engineer* IX (Jan. 3, 1884), p. 113.

European reaction to early skyscrapers, especially those of Chicago, is surveyed by Arnold Lewis in "The Disquieting Progress of Chicago," in *American Public Architecture,* ed. Craig Zabel and Susan Scott Munshower (University Park, Pa., 1989), pp. 114–37.

The tall office buildings of Chicago, Lewis writes on p. 121, were difficult to accept as architecture and "more menacing as a symbol of the power of speculation and its urban consequences for humans and for art." Also see Arnold Lewis, "A European Profile of American Architecture," *Journal of the Society of Architectural Historians* (*JSAH*) XXXVII (Dec. 1978), pp. 265–82.

13. Louis H. Sullivan, "The High-Building Question," the *Graphic* (Chicago) V (Dec. 19, 1891), p. 405. Also see my essay "The Setback Skyscraper City of 1891: An Unknown Essay by Louis H. Sullivan," *JSAH* XXIX (May 1970), pp. 181–87, with Sullivan's paper as an appendix.

The clamor to limit building heights in Chicago began as early as 1884 and was not always socially motivated; controls could protect the value of skyscrapers already built. See *Chicago Tribune,* May 18, 1890, p. 28.

"Like Frankenstein, we stand appalled before the monster of our own creation," the critic Montgomery Schuyler remarked in 1903; see *American Architecture and Other Writings by Montgomery Schuyler,* ed. William H. Jordy and Ralph Coe (Cambridge, Mass., 1961), vol. II, p. 445.

14. For typical allusions to Babel, see W. L. B. Jenney, "The Building Stones of Chicago," a speech of Nov. 27, 1883, at the Chicago Academy of Sciences, in *Engineering News* XI (Jan. 5, 1884), p. 1; Ferree, "The High Building and Its Art," p. 301; Frank Lloyd Wright, *Modern Architecture* (Princeton, N.J., 1931), p. 89; and Lewis Mumford, "Babel in Europe," in *The Highway and the City* (New York, 1964).

The necropolis metaphor was evoked by N. O. Nelson in 1901 (see John S. Garner, "Leclaire, Illinois: A Model Company Town [1890–1934]," *JSAH* XXX [Oct. 1971], p. 226); by Wright, *An Autobiography* (New York, 1943), pp. 499–500, in a campaign to limit skyscrapers in San Francisco (see *The Ultimate Highrise,* ed. Bruce Brugmann and Greggar Sletteland [San Francisco, 1971], p. 109); and in a 1968 montage by Claes Oldenburg, "Proposed for a Skyscraper for Michigan Avenue, Chicago in

and the 'Academic Tradition' of the Early Eighteen-Nineties," *Journal of the Warburg and Courtauld Institutes* VII (Jan.–June 1944), p. 55n, agrees that the Reliance Building was the best early scheme for a skyscraper; in *Architecture: Nineteenth and Twentieth Centuries*, 2nd ed. (Baltimore, 1963), p. 245, he calls it "a refined and perfected version of Holabird & Roche's Tacoma Building."

13. The *Economist* XII (Aug. 25, 1894), p. 206.

In reporting the informal opening of the building, the *Chicago Tribune*, March 16, 1895, p. 8, described it as a "glazed terra-cotta tower." The double-bay oriel on State Street, mostly the best glass, is 25 feet 10 inches wide.

14. Van Brunt, *Architecture and Society*, p. 187, and Sullivan, *The Autobiography of an Idea*, p. 183, and "The Tall Office Building Artistically Considered," p. 403.

Notes—Wright and Light

1. Wright, *An Autobiography* [1943], p. 123, and *Frank Lloyd Wright Preliminary Studies 1889–1916,* ed. Yukio Futagawa (Tokyo, 1985), pp. 12, 199.

2. If built, the Luxfer project would have been doubly commercial: a speculation in commercial real estate and an advertisement for a commercial product. Wright described it as "a front only" in *Architectural Forum* 68 (Jan. 1938), p. 54.

For an excellent account of the prism enterprise, see Dietrich Neumann, "'The Century's Triumph in Lighting': The Luxfer Prism Companies and Their Contribution to Early Modern Architecture," *JSAH* LIV (March 1995), pp. 24–53.

3. Wright, *Genius and the Mobocracy*, pp. 45, 40, and *Ausgeführte Bauten und Entwürfe von Frank Lloyd Wright* (Berlin, 1911), caption to plate XXXIII. Also see Jack Quinan, *Frank Lloyd Wright's Larkin Building* (Cambridge, Mass., 1987), and Clausen, "Frank Lloyd Wright, Vertical Space, and the Chicago School's Quest for Light," p. 73. The Larkin Building was addressed south, and the audience in Unity Temple, rather than facing east, also looked south and to the light.

4. See H. Austin Adams, *The Man John D. Spreckels* (San Diego, 1924), p. 293, and *Harper's Weekly* 58 (July 11, 1914), p. 29. Also see *San Francisco: Its Builders Past and Present* (Chicago, 1913), vol. 1, pp. 12–17; *Who's Who in America* VII (Chicago, 1912–13), p. 1976; Richard V. Dodge, *Rails of the Silver Gate: The Spreckels San Diego Empire* (San Marino, Calif., 1960), passim; and *San Francisco Chronicle*, Aug. 15, 1913, pp. 1, 2.

5. "John Lloyd Wright Mini-Library 1912–14," typescript in the Chicago Historical Society. Anthony Alofsin cited these papers in *Frank Lloyd Wright: The Lost Years, 1910–1922* (Chicago, 1993), p. 364n. Also see John Lloyd Wright, *My Father Who Is on Earth* [1946] (Dover reprint as *My Father, Frank Lloyd Wright*, New York, 1992), pp. 63–66, and Sally Kitt Chappell and Ann Van Zanten, *Barry Byrne, John Lloyd Wright: Architecture and Design* (Chicago, 1982), p. 44.

For the Workingmen's Hotel, see *Architect and Engineer* (of California) XXXIV (Aug. 1913), pp. 80–82. Albright had presented a paper on reinforced concrete construction as early as 1905, Bruce Kamerling notes in *Irving J. Gill, Architect* (San Diego, 1993), p. 19. Also see "A Concrete Protest by Harrison Albright," *Architect and Engineer* XXXIII (June 1913), p. 90.

6. Wright, "The Art and Craft of the Machine," *Catalogue of the Fourteenth Annual Exhibition of the Chicago Architectural Club* (Chicago, 1901), n.p., and A. O. Elzner, "The First Concrete Skyscraper," *Architectural Record* XV (June 1904), p. 533.

7. Ericsson, *Sixty Years a Builder* (Chicago, 1942), p. 288, and Sullivan, quoted in the *Kansas City Star,* June 17, 1906, p. 4. Sullivan was taken on a tour of Kansas City by the architect Walter C. Root, the younger brother of John Root.

The great earthquake caused the San Francisco water system to fail; see Stephen Tobriner, "The Phoenix Rising: San Francisco Confronts the Danger of Earthquake and Fire, 1906–1914," in *American Public Architecture*, pp. 184–205. For the proposal to build a new hotel in Tokyo, see Kathryn Smith, "Frank Lloyd Wright and the Imperial Hotel: A Postscript," *Art Bulletin* LXVII (June 1985), p. 297.

8. G. K. Gilbert et al., "The San Francisco Earthquake and Fire of April 18, 1906, and Their Effects on Structures and Structural Materials," *Geological Survey Bulletin No. 324* (Washington, D.C., 1907), p. 34, and Ernest L. Ransome and Alexis Saurbrey, *Reinforced Concrete Buildings* (New York, 1912), p. 6.

The concrete buildings at Stanford were the museum and Roble Hall, a women's dormitory; see Paul V. Turner, "The Collaborative Design of Stanford University," in *The Founders & the Architects* (Stanford, Calif., 1976), pp. 41, 43. Construction details of the nineteen-story Claus Spreckels Building were thoroughly published in *Engineering Record* XXXVII (April 9, 1898), pp. 412–14, and (April 16, 1898), pp. 433–35. Also see *San Francisco Call*, Aug. 17, 1895, p. 1, and *Building and Industrial News* XII (Jan. 2, 1912), p. 2.

9. *Frank Lloyd Wright in the Realm of Ideas,* ed. Bruce Brooks Pfeiffer and Gerald Nordland (Carbondale, Ill., 1988), p. 63.

Today the Claus Spreckels Building, drastically altered, is known as the Central Tower. Two reinforced concrete buildings of 1907–8 by Charles F. Whittlesey, who once worked for Sullivan, stand close by the site of Wright's project: the flatiron on the west side of Market and Ellis streets and the Pacific Building at the southwest corner of Fourth and Market streets. See Michael R. Corbett, *Splendid Survivors* (San Francisco, 1979), p. 89.

10. The plans as published in *Frank Lloyd Wright: The Life-Work of the American Architect* (Santpoort, Holland, 1925), p. 80, show that Wright later developed the approach to the main entrance.

For lot sizes along Market Street, see the Assessor's maps, vol. 25, block 3706. Wright's site would have been 170 feet deep, with a frontage of probably only 50 feet.

11. *Collected Writings*, vol. 1, p. 190, and Ransome and Saurbrey, *Reinforced Concrete Buildings,* p. 13.

The Imperial Hotel performed well in an earthquake on April 26, 1922, but suffered damage in the Great Kanto earthquake of Sept. 1, 1923, the day set for its opening; see Shinjiro Kirishiki, "The Story of the Imperial Hotel, Tokyo," *Japan Architect,* Jan.–Feb. 1968, p. 136. I am indebted to Edgar Tafel for this reference.

12. "Great Building for the Call," the *Call*, March 21, 1913, pp. 1, 2. The proposed building was to cost $1.5 million, and Spreckels was said to have paid $1.1 million for the site, which fronted 100 feet on Market Street. For this important source I am indebted to Prof. Dietrich Neumann of Brown University for sharing with me an undergraduate thesis by his student Christopher Murray, "Claus Spreckels and the Landscape of Capital" (April 1994). Also see the *Chronicle*, March 21, 1913, p. 16; the *Examiner,* March 21, 1913, p. 10, which reported it "the highest price ever recorded for Market Street frontage"; *Building and Industrial News* XIII (March 24, 1913), p. 8; and *Architect and Engineer* XXXII (April 1913), frontispiece.

For typical work by the Reid Bros. (James Reid and Merritt Reid), see *Architect and Engineer* XXIII (Nov. 1910), pp. 34–91, XXX (Sept. 1912), pp. 48, 68, and XXXI (Jan. 1913), p. 61; *Building and Industrial News* XII (Dec. 31, 1912), plate B, and XIII (Feb. 25, 1913), p. 11; and *American Architect and Building News* 87 (April 29, 1905), n.p.

13. The *Call*, Aug. 15, 1913, pp. 1, 2; the *Chronicle*, Aug. 15, 1913, pp. 1, 2; the *Call*, Aug. 27, 1913, pp. 1, 2, and Aug. 31, 1913, p. 11.

14. "John Lloyd Wright Mini-Library 1912–14," n.p. Wright was particularly fond of the model and installed it in his Taliesin studio as if it were a sculpture. A second model was made for his exhibition at the Museum of Modern Art in New York in 1940.

In a small perspective study for the *Call* project, Wright shows the connecting wing with a grand entrance arch decidedly reminiscent of the "Golden Door"; see Bruce Brooks Pfeiffer, *Frank Lloyd Wright Drawings* (New York, 1990), p. 108. Notes on the same drawing about window shades and sizes prove that he was still thinking about office lighting.

15. Wright, "Louis H. Sullivan, His Work," *Architectural Record* LVI (July 1924), p. 29. In 1956, when he announced his fantasy project for a skyscraper 5,280 feet tall served by nuclear-powered elevators, Wright called it a memorial first of all to "Louis H. Sullivan, son of Chicago. First made the tall building tall." See Pfeiffer, *Frank Lloyd Wright Drawings,* p. 117.

16. Wright, *Modern Architecture*, pp. 88, 98, 86, 85, and *Genius and the Mobocracy,* p. 59.

17. *Collected Writings*, vol. 1, p. 178.

"America was born to *destroy the façade* in all things, governmental or personal, that do not express the inner spirit," Wright declared in 1953; see *Collected Writings*, vol. 5, p. 67.

As to skyscrapers cloaked in masonry, he remarked the "contradiction of structure and idea: the tenuous open steel frame is, in character, the reverse of mass"; see *An Autobiography* [1932], in *Collected Writings*, vol. 2, p. 337.

Notes—Wright's Idea

1. Wright, in *Architectural Forum* 68 (Jan. 1938), p. 55. In *Architectural Record* 64 (Oct. 1928), p. 342, he poignantly related that he had shown his 1923 studies to Sullivan. "This design is dedicated to him," Wright wrote.

2. Esther McCoy, *Vienna to Los Angeles: Two Journeys* (Santa Monica, Calif., 1979), p. 138.

3. *The International Competition for a New Administration Building for the Chicago Tribune MCMXXII* (Chicago, 1923), passim.

4. Wright, *An Autobiography* [1943], p. 518. The top awards were $50,000, $20,000 and $10,000; each of the ten invited firms was awarded $2,000.

5. *Eric Mendelsohn: Letters of an Architect*, ed. Oskar Beyer (London, 1967), pp. 163, 167. Bruno Zevi, in *Erich Mendelsohn* (New York, 1985), p. 32, terms the 1919 sketch a "fantasy project." Mendelsohn lectured in Berlin in 1919 and spoke of the "new possibilities of construction using the new materials of glass, steel, and concrete"; see *Erich Mendelsohn: Complete Works of the Architect* [1930] (New York, 1992), p. 8.

6. Behrendt, "Skyscrapers in Germany," *Journal of the American Institute of Architects* XI (Sept. 1923), pp. 367–68. Behrendt objected to central light courts as causing "increased danger in case of fire." Also see Dietrich Neumann, "Three Early Designs by Mies van der Rohe," *Perspecta* 27 (1992), esp. pp. 77–90.

Ludwig Hilberseimer, a colleague of Mies at the Illinois Institute of Technology, in Chicago, wrote of the first skyscraper project (Mies's Friedrichstrasse competition entry): "It is the proper expression of a building completely sheathed in glass, whose structural principle is based on the mushroom type of reinforced concrete slab construction. The floors are carried on the central shafts from which each slab is cantilevered. As no bearing walls are needed on the perimeter of the slabs, the outer envelope of the building can logically be of glass." See his study, *Mies van der Rohe* (Chicago, 1956), p. 23.

7. Of course, by comparison to the "heavenly light" of the Gothic cathedrals, the great urban landmarks of the Middle Ages, the prominence of glass skyscrapers in our time testifies to the secularization of modern life.

8. McCoy, *Vienna to Los Angeles*, pp. 126–30. Schindler was especially impressed by the adobe pueblos of New Mexico, which he encountered in 1915 and considered "the first buildings in America which have a real feeling for the ground which carries them"; see McCoy, *Five California Architects*, p. 153. His 1915 project for an adobe country house in Taos appears much more relevant to Wright's conception of Hollyhock House than the sundry ceremonial power structures of the ancient Maya; see my study, *Frank Lloyd Wright's Hollyhock House* (New York, 1992), pp. 39, 41.

Schindler built his double studio-house at 835 N. Kings Road, only a block south of Gill's reinforced concrete house of 1914–16 for Walter Dodge; see Kathryn Smith, *R. M. Schindler House, 1921–22* (West Hollywood, Calif., 1987). Smith writes in *Frank Lloyd Wright, Hollyhock House and Olive Hill* (New York, 1992), p. 166, that Schindler worked evenings for Wright in Los Angeles during February and March 1923. Also see Kamerling, *Irving J. Gill*, p. 89.

9. Frank L. Meline was a realtor, subdivider, and developer who owned various other businesses in Los Angeles. For the Play Mart project, see *The Architectural Drawings of R. M. Schindler*, ed. David Gebhard, vol. 3 (New York, 1992). Gebhard, in *Schindler* (New York, 1972), p. 92, remarks that the bands of black glass and aluminum established the horizontal as "the dominant note."

10. *An Autobiography* [1932], in *Collected Writings*, vol. 2, p. 261.

11. "Experimenting With Human Lives" [1923], in *Collected Writings*, vol. 1, pp. 169, 171.

12. *Collected Writings*, vol. 1, pp. 174, 185–86.

13. *An Autobiography* [1932], in *Collected Writings*, vol. 2, p. 290; *An Autobiography* [1943], p. 254; "In the Cause of Architecture," *Architectural Record* 64 (Oct. 1928), pp. 335–36, 341, 338–40; and *An Autobiography* [1943], pp. 256–57.

14. "In the Cause of Architecture," *Architectural Record* 64 (July 1928), p. 11.

15. *An Autobiography* [1943], p. 258, and "In the Cause of Architecture," *Architectural Record* 64 (July 1928), pp. 15–16.

16. Johnson had announced in Jan. 1922 his proposal for a skyscraper on the same site (327 feet on Chestnut Street and 214 feet on Michigan Avenue) from plans by Graham, Anderson, Probst & White; see John W. Stamper, *Chicago's North Michigan Avenue* (Chicago, 1991), pp. 93–94.

As early as 1905 he had financed Scotty's chartering of a Santa Fe train to set a speed record of 44 hours and 54 minutes from Los Angeles to Chicago. "Scotty hasn't got a dime," Johnson testified many years later, when Scotty's wife sued for divorce and alimony. "I've been paying his bills for years." Scotty once rode through Manhattan on a buckboard with a keg of gold coins. See *New York Times*, Jan. 8, 1948, p. 25, and Jan. 6, 1954, p. 31; *Life* 36 (Jan. 18, 1954), p. 40; *Time* 63 (Jan. 18, 1954), p. 88; and Edward A. Vandeventer, "Death Valley Scotty, Mysterious Son of the Desert," *Sunset Magazine* 56 (March 1926), pp. 22–25.

17. McCoy, *Vienna to Los Angeles*, p. 140.

18. *Richard Neutra: Promise and Fulfillment, 1919–1932*, ed. Dione Neutra (Carbondale, Ill., 1986), pp. 126–28. Wright's project for Johnson's desert dwelling and Schindler's design of the J. C. Packard house in Pasadena, Calif., bear striking resemblances to each other; cf. *Frank Lloyd Wright Preliminary Studies 1917–1932*, ed. Yukio Futagawa (Tokyo, 1986), pp. 60–61, and McCoy, *Five California Architects*, pp. 162–63.

19. *An Autobiography* [1932], in *Collected Writings* vol. 2, pp. 291–93.

20. Ibid., p. 292.

21. Wright liked to say "there is nothing so timid as a million dollars," Alexander Woollcott wrote in "The Prodigal Father," *New Yorker* 6 (July 19, 1930), p. 22.

Lloyd Wright recalled that he too made a rendering of the project on Water Tower square; see David Gebhard and Harriette Von Breton, *Lloyd Wright, Architect* (Santa Barbara, Calif., 1971), p. 71. Charles Morgan's best-known work, designed in partnership with Robert De Golyer, was the Powhatan Apartment Building at 4950 South Chicago Beach Drive in Chicago.

Notes—The Anti-skyscraper

1. The other, Guthrie wrote, was his friend the "poet preacher" Alexis W. Stein, a clergyman whose untimely death of tuberculosis occurred in 1910; see W. S. Rainsford, "Alexis Stein," *Outlook* 96 (Oct. 1, 1910), pp. 281–83.

Guthrie wrote to console Wright after the tragedy at Taliesin in which the architect's companion, her two children, and four other persons were murdered by a deranged servant. He invited Wright to recuperate at a retreat in the mountains of Virginia.

2. Wright published a handsome perspective of the Guthrie house project as plate LXI of *Ausgeführte Bauten und Entwürfe von Frank Lloyd Wright*, and used the same design for the Frank J. Baker house in Wilmette, Ill. His description of Guthrie appears in a letter of Aug. 6, 1929. Guthrie wrote of Wright's "constant misrepresentation of Greek architecture" in a letter of Feb. 20, 1928, and about his own readings in aesthetics on March 11, 1929.

3. Letter dated Nov. 12, 1928; an undated letter; "Discussion Shakes the Churches," *Current Opinion* 76 (Feb. 1924), p. 211; and the letter of March 11, 1929.

4. *Frank Lloyd Wright Preliminary Studies 1917–1932*, pp. 132–33.

5. *About Wright*, ed. Edgar Tafel (New York, 1993), p. 96.

6. "Report of the Properties Committee, St. Mark's in-the-Bouwerie, New York City, Referring to Plot Plan of Our Block," Dec. 11, 1929, passim. Of those seventeen properties the church today owns only the rectory.

7. *Architectural Forum* 68 (Jan. 1938), p. 54. Premature publicity in both *Time* XIV (Oct. 28, 1929), p. 62, and *Outlook and Independent* 153 (Oct. 30, 1929), p. 336, focused on the "inverted pyramids" Wright had designed for St. Mark's. To the degree that Wright's design defied gravity, it deliberately emphasized the non-masonry wall.

The notion that the towers would wash clean in the rain echoed the optimism of an early description of the enameled terra cotta facing planned for the Reliance Building: "It will be washed by every rainstorm," the *Economist* XII (Aug. 25, 1894), p. 206, reported.

8. *An Autobiography* [1932], in *Collected Writings,* vol. 2, p. 349; "The New Larkin Administration Building," in Quinan, *Frank Lloyd Wright's Larkin Building,* p. 141; and *Collected Writings,* vol. 1, p. 322. In *An Autobiography* [1943], p. 343, Wright refers to the St. Mark's project as an alternative to "false masonry-mass."

9. *Architectural Forum* 68 (Jan. 1938), p. 54, and *An Autobiography* [1932], in *Collected Writings,* vol. 2, p. 349. Those who exaggerate the value of the hearth as a symbol of family life commonly ignore Wright's withdrawal of the masonry masses to admit more daylight. (They also overlook the fact that he was hardly an exemplar of family values.) "The masonry chimney masses," he noted of his House on the Mesa project of 1932, "are all used for anchorage and support to secure the cantilevers and leave the main walls entirely free." See *Collected Writings,* vol. 3, p. 129.

In respect to lateral stresses from wind loads, the structural idea of St. Mark's Tower could also be regarded as a vertical cantilever anchored in the earth.

When *Architectural Record* 67 (Jan. 1930), pp. 1–4, published the St. Mark's project with color illustrations, Wright evidently supplied such comments as "Located in a park on church property these towers will always stand free."

The implications of decentralization relate to his prediction in "Experimenting With Human Lives" [1923], in *Collected Writings,* vol. 1, p. 172: "Modern transportation may scatter the city, open breathing spaces in it, green it, and beautify it, making it fit for a superior order of human beings."

10. Wright, letter of Nov. 9, 1929 to Justin L. Miner.

Various factors coalesced to dissuade the vestry from proceeding with St. Mark's Tower. A "crisis" of premature publicity, most of it generated of course by Wright, led property owners to raise the prices of the lots St. Mark's hoped to acquire. One vestryman called Wright "a prima donna with press bureau," Guthrie wrote on Feb. 22, 1930. The church in any event lacked funds to buy all the necessary properties, Warren Matthews wrote on March 11, 1930. Both the Depression and the condition of the St. Mark's neighborhood lowered the potential rent schedule. Guthrie, in a letter of April 23, 1930, said the plans would need to be changed to make the bedrooms acceptable "to the sort of tenants we can have." In March 1930, Wright estimated that the eighteen-story tower would cost only $480,000 furnished and would generate a net return of at least 13 percent. The church estimated costs of $700,000 and a return of only 6 percent.

11. *The Story of the Tower* [1956], in *Collected Writings,* vol. 5, pp. 150, 153, and "Personal Commentary by Frank Lloyd Wright," dedication program, Feb. 9, 1956, n.p.

Sullivan, in *The Autobiography of an Idea,* p. 313, had argued that when tall office buildings "are crowded together upon narrow streets or lanes they become mutually destructive."

12. *The Story of the Tower* (New York, 1956), pp. 8, 9, and Harold Price, Jr., interview with Sue Lacy, Feb. 24, 1990, quoted by permission of the Landmark Preservation Council of Bartlesville, Okla.

In looking at Goff's drawings, Wright told Joe Price that the house was unbuildable because it was not planned on the module, Goff related in a conversation of Dec. 1962. Wright had the decency, at least, to tell Goff directly how much he disliked the "travesty"; see David G. De Long, *Bruce Goff* (Cambridge, Mass., 1988), p. 126. Goff responded by producing a second scheme for the house employing an equilateral triangle as a module in all three dimensions.

13. *The Story of the Tower,* p. 9.

14. Wright, *Sixty Years of Living Architecture,* series 9 (Chicago, 1956), n.p.

15. "Personal Commentary by Frank Lloyd Wright," n.p., and Besinger, *Working with Mr. Wright* (Cambridge, England, 1995), p. 243.

In a letter of Oct. 27, 1952, Price agreed to enlarge the plan of the tower from a 42-foot square to a 46-foot square. George C. Nimmons, in "Skyscrapers in America," p. 370, had asserted: "Irregular shaped offices, or living rooms for that matter, are contrary to the human housing instinct, difficult for the arrangement of furniture, expensive to construct and very wasteful in space by reason of the irregular unusable corners."

16. From the top of the tower a finial known as the "light-needle" rose 30 feet higher. The eighteen-story version of St. Mark's Tower would have been 205 feet 3 inches tall. Price wrote Wright, on Dec. 27, 1955, that there was too much sunlight in the northwest quadrant. He also found the narrow and angled apartment stairs to be slippery and "very dangerous."

In the project for St. Mark's Tower, the spandrels were to have been of copper rather than concrete faced with copper. Aluminum, unfortunately, was substituted for bronze in the sashes of the Price Tower.

INDEX

A. T. Stewart Store, 11
Ackerman, James S., 87
Adler, Dankmar, 5, 9, 16, 24, 37, 41, 83–87
Adler & Sullivan, 5, 6, 22–24, 83, 86
Albright, Harrison, 41, 51, 88
Aldis, Owen F., 5, 9, 14, 84, 86
Allen, Henry J., house, 43
Alofsin, Anthony, 83
Andrew, David S., 85, 87
Auditorium building, 21, 40, 85

Baker, Frank J., residence, 89
Barnsdall, Aline, 53, 54
Baumann, Frederick, 9, 84
Bayard building, 86
Behrendt, Walker Curt, 53–55, 89
Besinger, Curtis, 75, 90
Bijvoet, Bernard, 53
Bletter, Rosemarie, 86
Borden Block, 17, 37, 87
Bourget, Paul, 8, 84
Bragdon, Claude, 83, 85–87
Brooks, Peter C., 9, 84
Brooks, Shepherd, 83
Bruegmann, Robert, 84
Bryan, John A., 86
Burnham, Daniel, 5, 32, 86
Burnham & Root, 5, 6, 9, 10, 13, 23, 40,
    83, 84, 86

Call building, 44, 48, 49, 51, 88
Catlin, Daniel, 21
Chamber of Commerce building, 6
Chappell, Sally Kitt, 88
Chicago Tribune competition, 53, 89
Claus Spreckels building, 48, 49, 51, 88
Clausen, Meredith L., 84, 88
"Commercial Arts Festival" project, 63
"Commercial building in Copper,
    Concrete and Glass," 55
Condit, Carl W., 83, 84, 86
Corbett, Michael R., 88
Cox, James, 87
Cummings & Sears, Architects, 23

De Golyer, Robert, 89
De Long, David G., 90
de Young, M. H., 51

Dodge, Walter, residence, 89
Dooly Block, 24
Duiker, Johannes, 53
Duskin, Alvin, 83

Edbrooke, George H., 10, 84
Edelmann, John, 10, 18, 22, 37, 83, 86, 87
Elmslie, George Grant, 85, 87
Elstein, Rochelle S., 87
Elzner, A. O., 88
Ericsson, Henry, 48, 84, 88

Fagin building, 13
Ferree, Barr, 7, 83, 85, 87
Filler, Martin, 85
Flinn, John J., 40, 87
Frank Meline Co., 55
Friedrichstrasse competition, 89

Garner, John S., 83
Gebhard, David, 89
Geraniotis, Roula Mouroudellis, 84, 86
Getty Tomb, 21
Giedion, Sigfried, 87
Gill, Irving J., 48, 55, 88, 89
Goff, Bruce, 72, 90
Gould, Jay, 21
Grannis, Amos, 83
Grannis Block, 6
Gregersen, Charles, 84
Gropius, Walter, 53
Guaranty building, 21, 85
Guthrie, William Norman, 63–65, 71, 89,
    90

Hale, William E., 5, 83
Hamlin, A. D. F., 7, 83
Haren, William A., 23, 86
Heath, William, 44
Hilberseimer, Ludwig, 89
Hitchcock, Henry-Russell, 84, 86, 87
Holabird & Roche, 10, 14, 53, 88
Home Insurance building, 10
Hood, Raymond, 53
Hotel del Coronado, 47, 51
House on the Mesa project, 90
Houser building, 23
Howells, John Mead, 53

Imperial Hotel, 50, 55, 64, 88
Ingalls building, 48
Insurance Exchange, 23

J. C. Packard house, 89
Jenney, William Le Baron, 10, 59, 83, 84
Johnson, Albert M., 57, 59, 61, 89
Jordy, William H., 86

Kamerling, Bruce, 88
Kellogg, F. W., 51
Kerr, Robert, 7, 8, 83
Kimball, Fiske, 84
Kirishiki, Shinjiro, 88

Landau, Sarah Bradford, 83, 84
Lane, M. A., 84
Larkin building, 43, 44, 55, 70, 88
Larson, Gerald R., 83, 84, 86
Leiter building, 10, 84
Lewis, Arnold, 83, 86
Loos, Adolf, 54
Luxfer Prisms project, 43, 68, 84, 88

Marshall Field Wholesale Store, 11, 37, 84,
    87
Masonic Temple, 6, 50, 87
Matthews, Warren Shepard, 65, 90
May, Clifford, 71
McCoy, Esther, 89
Meline, Frank J., 89
Mendelsohn, Erich, 53, 89
Menocal, Narciso G., 87
Meyer, Adolf, 53
Michelangelo Buonarroti, 39
Mies van der Rohe, Ludwig, 53, 85, 89
Milan, Cathedral of, 39
Milliken, Foster, 86
Miner, Justin, 71, 90
Monadnock building, 40, 41, 84, 86, 87
Montauk Block, 84
Moore, Charles, 86
Morgan, Charles, 61, 89
Morrison, Hugh, 87
Mueller, Paul, 5
Mujica, Francisco, 83, 84
Mumford, Lewis, 83, 84, 87
Mundie, William B., 59

Murray, Christopher, 88

National Life Insurance Co., 57, 64, 70, 80, 89
Nelson, N. O., 83
Neumann, Dietrich, 84, 88, 89
Neutra, Dione, 59, 89
Neutra, Richard, 54, 59, 89
Nimmons, George C., 86, 90

Oak Park studio, 43, 83
"Ocatilla" camp, 65, 68
Odd Fellows Temple, 6, 86
O'Gorman, James F., 84
Oldenburg, Claes, 83
Olive Hill residence, 53, 54, 89
Olmsted, Frederick Law, 7, 83
Owings building, 6

Phenix building, 23
Phoenix Iron Co., 25
Play Mart project, 55, 89
Powhatan apartment building, 89
Price, Harold C., 71–73
Price, Harold C. Jr., 71, 72, 90
Price, Joe, 71, 72, 90
Price Tower, 71–81, 90
Prudential building, see Guaranty building
Purdy, Corydon T., 9, 25, 34, 84, 86, 87

Quigley Memorial Seminary, 60
Quinan, Jack, 88, 90

Raeder & Ramsey, Architects, 22
Ramsey, Charles K., 22–24, 86
Randall, Frank A., 84
Randall, John D., 86
Ransome, Ernest L., 49, 51, 88
Reid Bros. (James and Merritt Reid), 51, 88
Reliance building, 5, 41, 42, 83, 87, 88, 90
Richardson, Henry Hobson, 11, 13, 37, 54, 87

Robinson, Cervin, 84
Rookery, The, 13, 14, 84
Root, John Wellborn, 5, 6, 15–16, 24, 32, 41, 86–88
Root, Walter C., 88
Ruskin, John, 17, 18, 85, 87
Ryerson Tomb, 21

Saarinen, Eliel, 53
St. Mark's in-the-Bouwerie, 63, 90
St. Mark's Tower, 63–72, 90
San Marcos in the Desert, 65, 68
Saurbrey, Alexis, 88
Schiller Theater building, 37, 43, 86, 87
Schindler, R. M., 53–55, 89
Schuyler, Montgomery, 32, 83, 86, 87
Scott, Walter, 59, 89
Scully, Vincent, 86, 87
Semper, Gottfried, 9
Shillaber building, 22
Shultz, Earle, 85
Simmons, Walter, 85
Sistine Chapel, 39
Smith, Kathryn, 88, 89
Sprague, Paul, 86
Spreckels, Claus, 44
Spreckels, John D., 44, 47, 48, 51, 88
Stein, Alexis W., 89
Stewart, A. T., 11
Sullivan, Louis Henry, passim
Summerson, John, 85
Szarkowski, John, 86

Tacoma building, 6, 14, 15, 41, 84, 88
Taliesin, 47, 53, 54, 59, 64, 71, 80, 89
Tallmadge, Thomas E., 84
Theatre building, 48
Tobriner, Stephen, 88
Transportation building, World's Columbian Exposition (1893), 52, 88
Turner, Frederick Jackson, 18, 19, 85
Turner, Paul V., 88
Twombly, Robert, 85

Unity Temple, 44, 48, 88

Van Brunt, Henry, 15, 42, 84, 86–88
van Leeuwen, Thomas A. P., 87
van Rensselaer, Mrs. Schuyler (Mariana van Rensselaer), 87
Van Zanten, Ann, 88
Van Zanten, David, 87
Von Breton, Harriette, 89

Wainwright building, 3, 5, 6, 21–37, 40, 41, 43, 44, 52, 61, 83–87
Wainwright, Catherine D., 21–24, 85, 86
Wainwright, Charlotte Dickson, 24, 86
Wainwright, Ellis, 21, 22, 85, 86
Wainwright Real Estate Co., 23
Wainwright, Samuel, 21
Wainwright Tomb, 21, 24, 86
Walker, Donald, 64
Walker, Wirt D., 14
Walker building, 21
Weisman, Winston, 84
Whitman, Walt, 85
Whittlesey, Charles F., 88
Willis, Carol, 83
Willoughby, Charles L., 10
Willoughby building, 10, 11, 30, 84
Woman's Temple, 6
Workingmen's Hotel, 48, 88
Wotton, Henry, 84
Wright, Frank Lloyd, passim
Wright, John, 47, 48, 51, 52, 88
Wright, Lloyd, 48, 53, 89

Zabel, Craig, 85
Zajonc, Arthur, 84
Zevi, Bruno, 89